Nature, Spirituality, and Early Childhood Education

This novel volume delves into a specific and crucial aspect of early years pedagogy – the intersection between early childhood education and spirituality, offering tips on nurturing spirituality and a sense of connectedness with nature through outdoor learning.

With experience both as a scholar and a teacher, the author delves into the ontological and epistemological issues related to outdoor learning and education while keeping accessibility and sustainability at the centre of the volume. Chapters take a comprehensive approach to the exploration of children's innate spirituality and their connection with nature in the context of early childhood education, fusing elements such as a critique of early years policy with philosophy of education and children's mental health. Using a robust theoretical foundation incorporating philosophical figures such as Froebel, McMillan, Montessori, Dewey and Freire, as well as the inclusion of practical examples from educational settings designed for real-world scenarios, this book reinvigorates the conversation around the holistic development of children by emphasising the importance of nature and child-centred pedagogies.

Ultimately exploring avenues that can foster a sense of well-being and social responsibility in children, the book will be of interest to researchers, educators and teacher trainers in the field of early childhood education, environmental education, philosophy of education and teacher education. Policy makers and school leaders may also benefit from this volume.

Ruth Wills is a Lecturer in Early Childhood in the School of Education, Liverpool Hope University, UK, and a part-time teacher in a Primary School.

Routledge Research in Early Childhood Education

This series provides a platform for researchers to present their latest research and discuss key issues in Early Childhood Education.

Books in the series include:

The Yew Chung Approach to Early Childhood Education
Centering Emergent Curriculum, Child-Led Inquiry, and Multilingualism
Stephanie C. Sanders-Smith, Sylvia Ya-Hsuan Yang, and Kutasha Bryan-Silva

The Glocalization of Early Childhood Curriculum
Global Childhoods, Local Curricula
Philip Hui Li and Jennifer J. Chen

International Perspectives on Educating for Democracy in Early Childhood
Recognizing Young Children as Citizens
Edited by Stacy Lee DeZutter

School Children as Agents of Change
Raising up Critical Thinking and Judgment in the Early Years
Edited by Emanuela Guarcello and Abele Longo

Children's Voice and Agency in Diverse Settings
International Research and Perspectives
Edited by Mhairi C. Beaton, Anne Burke, Pigga Keskitalo and Tuija Turunen

School Children and the Challenge of Managing AI Technologies
Fostering a Critical Relationship through Aesthetic Experiences
Edited by Emanuela Guarcello and Abele Longo

Nature, Spirituality, and Early Childhood Education
Fostering Children's Awareness and Responsibility through Outdoor Learning
Ruth Wills

For more information about this series, please visit: https://www.routledge.com/Routledge-Research-in-Early-Childhood-Education/book-series/RRECE

Nature, Spirituality, and Early Childhood Education
Fostering Children's Awareness and Responsibility through Outdoor Learning

Ruth Wills

LONDON AND NEW YORK

First published 2025
by Routledge
4 Park Square, Milton Park, Abingdon, Oxon OX14 4RN

and by Routledge
605 Third Avenue, New York, NY 10158

Routledge is an imprint of the Taylor & Francis Group, an informa business

© 2025 Ruth Wills

The right of Ruth Wills to be identified as author of this work has been asserted in accordance with sections 77 and 78 of the Copyright, Designs and Patents Act 1988.

All rights reserved. No part of this book may be reprinted or reproduced or utilised in any form or by any electronic, mechanical, or other means, now known or hereafter invented, including photocopying and recording, or in any information storage or retrieval system, without permission in writing from the publishers.

Trademark notice: Product or corporate names may be trademarks or registered trademarks, and are used only for identification and explanation without intent to infringe.

British Library Cataloguing-in-Publication Data
A catalogue record for this book is available from the British Library

Library of Congress Cataloging-in-Publication Data
Names: Wills, Ruth, author.
Title: Nature, spirituality, and early childhood education: fostering children's awareness and responsibility through outdoor learning / Ruth Wills.
Description: Abingdon, Oxon; New York, NY: Routledge, 2025. | Series: Routledge research in early childhood education | Includes bibliographical references and index. | Summary: "This novel volume delves into a specific and crucial aspect of early years pedagogy - the intersection between early childhood education and spirituality, offering tips on nurturing spirituality and a sense of connectedness with nature through outdoor learning. With experience both as a scholar and a teacher, the author delves into the ontological and epistemological issues related to outdoor learning and education while keeping accessibility and sustainability at the centre of the volume.
Chapters take a comprehensive approach to the exploration of children's innate spirituality and their connection with nature in the context of early childhood education, fusing elements such as a critique of early years policy with philosophy of education and children's mental health. Using a robust theoretical foundation incorporating philosophical figures such as Froebel, McMillan, Montessori, Dewey and Freire, as well as the inclusion of practical examples from educational settings designed for real-world scenarios, this book reinvigorates the conversation around the holistic development of children by emphasizing the importance of nature and child-centred pedagogies. Ultimately exploring avenues that can foster a sense of well-being and social responsibility in children, the book will be of interest to researchers, educators and teacher trainers in the field of early childhood education, environmental education, philosophy of education and teacher education. Policy makers and school leaders may also benefit from this volume"– Provided by publisher.
Identifiers: LCCN 2024019332 (print) | LCCN 2024019333 (ebook) | ISBN 9781032749877 (hardback) | ISBN 9781032775937 (paperback) | ISBN 9781003483939 (ebook)
Subjects: LCSH: Early childhood education–Psychological aspects. | Nature study. | Spirituality–Study and teaching (Early childhood)
Classification: LCC LB1139.23 .W567 2025 (print) | LCC LB1139.23 (ebook) | DDC 372.21–dc23/eng/20240613
LC record available at https://lccn.loc.gov/2024019332
LC ebook record available at https://lccn.loc.gov/2024019333

ISBN: 978-1-032-74987-7 (hbk)
ISBN: 978-1-032-77593-7 (pbk)
ISBN: 978-1-003-48393-9 (ebk)

DOI: 10.4324/9781003483939

Typeset in Times New Roman
by Deanta Global Publishing Services, Chennai, India

This book is dedicated to the memory of Dr. Babs Anderson, a real Early Childhood pioneer whose legacy will last for many years to come.

It is also dedicated to the memory of Jonray and Ben – members of the class that taught me how to teach. Both gone too soon.

Contents

	Acknowledgements	*viii*
	Preamble: Children's spirituality in the outdoor space: Seven vignettes	1
1	Children's spirituality, nature and Early Childhood policy	9
2	Children's spirituality, nature and frameworks of understanding	24
3	Children's spirituality, nature and Early Childhood foundations	41
4	Children's spirituality, nature and Early Childhood practice	54
5	Children's spirituality, nature and pedagogy	70
6	Children's spirituality and nature: Recommendations for policy and practice	83
	Index	*89*

Acknowledgements

I would like to acknowledge the role that the children in the Reception class at my school have played in inspiring me to write this book. Thank you also to Zoe and Polly for catching the vision, and for the years of encouragement and support.

Thank you to my colleagues at Liverpool Hope University, and friends in the International Association for Children's Spirituality, all of whom have encouraged me in my thinking and doing.

Finally, I hope this book keeps the conversation on children, spirituality and nature alive – for the benefit of future generations of active learners and the sustaining of our precious planet.

Preamble
Children's spirituality in the outdoor space: Seven vignettes

Introduction

This book is inspired by my experience of working with a class of four and five-year-old children in a Primary school in England. On a Friday afternoon, whatever the weather, the children put on wellington boots, coats, gloves, woolly hats or sunhats to access the outdoor learning space termed 'The Lodge.' At the lodge, a large shed homes a range of resources for children's learning through play such as spades and rakes, kitchen equipment, clay, musical instruments, balls and scooters. The area surrounding the shed consists of a large expanse of grass, trees and bushes, with large tyres, pallets, tubes and a quiet corner. There is also a mud kitchen, where the children can get messy whilst using their imaginations in creating interesting concoctions and recipes. Children take part in free play in this area, choosing their resources and tidying away afterwards, and whilst two staff members are on duty to supervise and ensure safety, there is little adult intervention as the children work in small groups or individually, in a free flow of activity.

From observing the children at play in nature, it has become apparent to me that hallmarks of what I understand as the spiritual are present within the children's actions, responses and behaviours. For me, spirituality is about connections made with the self, others and environment that facilitate an exploration of who children are in relation to the world. It is also about inspiring a sense of wonder and awe. This, in turn can evoke an awareness of the dimension that goes beyond immediate consciousness and sometimes cannot be explained; for some, this will be transformational as awareness in the present is given meaning and purpose in the light of the transcendent.

A more detailed understanding of what is meant by spirituality will be explored in due course. However, it is important to note at the outset that spirituality in this context is considered as a trans-religious phenomenon which is intrinsic to all human beings of all ages and all cultural contexts (Harris, 2016). It concerns both everyday and transcendent experiences. Considering our existence *within* the world, spirituality involves a sense of how we relate to ourselves, others, the world and God (Hay & Nye, 2006), including identity and belonging (Eaude, 2023), relationships (de Souza, 2010) and a sense of

DOI: 10.4324/9781003483939-1

purpose (Benson et al., 2012). As Tang (2022, n.p.) suggests, a child's spirituality allows them 'to show awareness and consciousness of the surrounding worlds through curiosity, wonder, a sense of compassion and love.'

Yet, spirituality also might provide the inspiration for transcendence as an experience that takes us *beyond* the immediate. As will be explored in due course, I suggest that children's spirituality, with its range of expressions, can lead children to responsible action for their own transformation and that of wider local and global communities. At the outset of this book however, I provide examples representing actual events that illustrate how learning in nature contributes to children's spiritual awareness, and through each, it is hoped that a sense of the spiritual might be stimulated for readers – practitioners, students, academics and policy makers alike.

Imagination

On a cold sunny day in December, a small group of children use rakes and spades to dig through the dry fallen leaves and soily ground. Once the ground is cleared, they start to dig a hole. They want to dig all the way to Australia where it is warmer at this time of year. In the quiet corner, another small group of children have set up a cafe space. Laying a table on the ground using a waterproof mat, and cups and plates found in the shed, they work in the mud kitchen with pans and other tools, using the fallen leaves to create amazing recipes such as soup, coffee, pasta sauce and hot chocolate. They invite guests to the café who then must pay £9 for something to eat or drink! At the edge of the school field is an opening in the bushes. The children ask to explore. At the end of the session, the teacher leads the class single file along a 'trail' through the bushes, during which they must bend down, climb over and push through branches, leaves and foliage. On this short journey, the children imagine who might live here and look out for what they might find. They are also careful not to wake anybody up or disturb anyone who might be hiding. Each child has a story to tell and they are full of excitement as they share their ideas on the way back to the classroom. Their imaginations take them away from their immediate reality and allow them to explore a dimension beyond.

Presence

As the class busy themselves with their first chosen activity for the afternoon, with their excitement at being outside and free to choose tangible, one child who is non-verbal with a cognitive disability is quietly present as they look closely at leaves on a bush. Through this mindful activity of careful observation, as well as touching and feeling the texture of the leaves and smelling its specific scent, the child is present to self and the world. The chatter and laughter of the other children are merely a background buzz as the intense engagement with the leaves in the moment signifies the child's innate connection with the natural environment.

Creativity

On a warmer day, the children can be less physical to engage in more relaxing, mindful activities. A wooden pallet becomes an artist's easel, on which they draw, explore colour and make shapes with big chunky colourful chalks. Each child lies down on or kneels in front of the pallet and is quietly focused on creating something beautiful. Other children use musical instruments to explore sound and imitate the sounds heard in the environment such as birdsong, fluttering leaves and the wind in the trees. On another occasion, the children learn that by crushing soil and grass into a piece of cloth and then shaking it out, they can create a piece of artwork using natural colours from the earth. The teacher says that this could be the inspiration for a piece of music too. Creativity opens up possibilities and allows for the children to make personal responses to what they can see, hear and feel from within the natural environment.

Wonder

Being winter in the UK, as well as many fallen leaves, the trees also have shed their branches, with large and small twigs strewn over the outdoor learning space. Following a recent storm, with a tree having fallen in the outdoor area, sticks much bigger than the children lie on the ground. One child picks up such a stick to see how it might be balanced and carried. The look of joy on their face indicates pleasure in being successful in this activity. The child continues to provide a personal challenge, this time attempting to balance the long stick on the high branches of the tree in front of the shed. The child exclaims 'wow!' at which the other children join in, amazed to see this branch hanging from the tree. Eyes wide open, the child cannot take away this gaze of wonder. Later, the branch, and other logs, twigs and leaves are nailed together to form a sculpture.

On the same day, another child finds a long tube. It is propped up on a large tyre to make a slope and the child goes into the shed to find some balls. The idea is to see which balls are faster. A group of children jump up and down with excitement when the balls run quickly down the tube and out of the other end. This experiment however results in the hypothesis not being quite right. It is the bigger ball that is faster. The look of wonder on this child's face shows how they are thinking about why this might be the case before the experiment is repeated, just to make sure. Wonder inspires curiosity and questioning. It also promotes a sense of how the world works, and often through such experiences, children can evaluate the role of their existence within it.

4 *Preamble*

Individuality and connectedness

Some children like to play alone. The outdoor space allows for them to explore, think, experiment and reflect. Some enjoy spending time walking around and listening to sounds in the environment such as birds and aeroplanes. Some enjoy making a den to sit in or creating an obstacle course which takes them into their own secret world of imagination and reflection. Sometimes they share their thoughts with others, but often the activity is personal to them. Individual activity is not always reflective, however. It can also serve to develop or inspire individual skills and interests. One child spent a whole session attempting to master balance on a scooter without the use of stabilisers. Another categorised leaves into colour shades, making a set of colour-coded piles. A child with minimal speech identified objects in the sky and on the ground (bird; plane; stick) whilst another climbed on the fallen tree to see how far they could go without feeling scared.

On the other hand, the open space affords an opportunity for children to collaborate and connect inter-personally without the physical limitations of the classroom. The more active children enjoy climbing up onto a large tyre and although a ladder is in place, there is always someone who needs help to get up and down. The small tractors, scooters and bikes are always popular, but the children know that they need to help each other to move them across the bumpy grass to get to the tarmacked area which is smoother and easier for movement. The football pitch is also popular but again the children need to work together to set rules and boundaries in the absence of a referee or staff member to supervise specifically. Further to this, at 'The Lodge,' there is no visible division of gender, culture, ability or disability. Although the class is representative of difference, the outdoor activities, which are undertaken on children's own terms, do not exclude.

Corporeal experience

All activities at 'The Lodge' have a dimension of corporeality. Children learn through practical activity within an embodied pedagogy that involves the senses, emotions and physicality. Everything is 'hands-on' and whether running, balancing, digging, drawing, climbing, smelling, observing, cycling, acting, kicking, storytelling or music-making, their learning is holistic, drawing on their physical and emotional potential. During 'Lodge' sessions, children always try out new things. This was evidenced one day when they asked to play by the fallen tree. Under the supervision of two staff members, this became their new playground. Each engaged with this 'equipment' in a unique way, but equally each child tried out something new based on their own interests, be they climbing up and along the tree trunk, counting the number of leaves on the tree, acting out a drama using the branches and fallen twigs, exploring which branches were most bouncy or using it as an obstacle course. In some cases there was an element of risk involved, but in each case this unplanned session catered for as many aspects of the early years curriculum as there are boxes to tick. This is an example of the richness of the outdoor space not only for children's learning and development, but an indication also of how the personal and social dimension of education is inherent within their experiences of nature.

Care

Every so often, the children have a visitor to school. The guinea pig belonging to a staff member sometimes makes an appearance for Friday afternoon fun. The children stroke him and hold him. One child describes how this makes them feel less sad. One Friday afternoon in early spring, it is warm enough to take the guinea pig to 'The Lodge.' The children are tasked with making a 'theme park' for him – an area in which he can play and explore. A small group of children is involved in this activity but at the same time, another group, in a different area, dig a hole and fill it with leaves, to become a bed so that he can relax after playing. One child also is concerned that he will need his water bottle, so using the engineering skills of a four-year-old, works out how to prop up the water bottle so that the guinea pig can drink. The children are very considerate of his needs, as well as gentle when handling him. One child says that tonight's dreams will be about animals.

Children's spirituality: an introduction

The categories presented in these vignettes, whilst certainly not exhaustive, are included in a long list of personal and social human attributes considered spiritual in children's spirituality literature. As Hay and Nye (2006) suggest, an awareness of wonder, for example, in seeing a waterfall or sunset, is characteristic of an aesthetic appreciation of the natural world. This might inspire a sense of mystery and contemplation, within or devoid of any religious framework. For other scholars, spirituality involves connectedness leading to a sense of unity of self and other (de Souza, 2010); it can inspire a corporeal dimension of knowing (physical and emotional) within everyday life (Hyde, 2008) and it relates to a sense of self as part of something greater (Adams et al., 2008).

Spirituality inspires imagination (Mountain, 2007), provides a space for personal reflection and leads to existential questioning (Webster, 2004). Spirituality is related to play which inspires creativity and critical thinking, and through this, children might negotiate ideas about identity, culture and society (Goodliff, 2013). It also concerns well-being, including fostering an emerging sense of self and happiness (Erricker, 2009). Finally, spirituality might again be exercised through play, additionally providing opportunities for children to experience moments of wonder, awe, joy and inner peace (Mata-McMahon et al., 2019; Mata-McMahon & Escarfuller, 2023).

The highlighting of categories of children's spirituality here is predicated on a belief that taking learning outdoors might inspire an awareness of something both within and beyond their ordinary experience (McCreery, 1996). In comparison to the activities undertaken by young children within an increasingly performative outworking of Early Childhood curricula (Carroll-Meehan et al., 2024), learning outdoors has the potential to promote what is termed by Hay and Nye (2006) as awareness sensing. This might not be easily articulated, described or measured, but certainly has personal significance for learners.

Concluding comment

At a time when environmental concerns and mental health issues seem to dominate political and media-driven conversations, as suggested above, Early Childhood Education in many countries is currently experiencing a move towards a more technocratic paradigm of education. Where outdoor work, play and creativity have historically been staple components of a child-led pedagogy, there is evidence across the globe that the more performative and measurable aspects of learning are now being prioritised (Carrol-Meehan et al., 2024). However, in the light of my experiences in school, illustrated by the vignettes above, I have identified how the more informal practices listed here can contribute tangibly to children's sense of personal and social identity, physical development and well-being. For young children experiencing education during their formative period of development and personal growth, this forms the basis for future learning.

Following this, we might consider the value of learning outdoors for positive well-being, and indeed it is possible to deduce that the scenarios above illustrate children's various expressions of well-being. However it is somewhat reductionist to limit spirituality to well-being alone. The idea here that spiritual awareness inspired by outdoor learning should not only be an experience 'in-itself' (Hegel, 1977) but manifest in action. The overall question to be considered is this: how might young children's spirituality inspire a sense of well-being and social responsibility in response to their experience of nature?

It is thus my conjecture that the innate spiritual sense that children have can inspire them to experience an awareness *beyond* themselves. In this text, it is stressed that spiritual awareness and development do not end with the immediate self or even the relationship between self and others. Rather, based on their experiences in nature, young children might extend and develop their learning and meaning-making to influence their attitudes and behaviour towards local and global 'others.' With the help of their supporting adults, within an environment and culture of schooling that promotes active listening and response to children's reactions to their learning (Pramling Samuelsson, 2011), the very young can commit to sustainable action or promote welcome and inclusion.

Whilst offering a narrative that sits within the Critical Pedagogy approach, the intention in this book is not to negate or critique the paradigm of performativity, as this is the daily experience for many of us in practice. Rather, the aim is to explore how learning outdoors might inspire a dimension of engagement *beyond* this paradigm for enhanced well-being and a greater awareness of others and the world.

References

Adams, K., Hyde, B. & Woolley, R. (2008). *The spiritual dimension of childhood*. London: Jessica Kingsley.

Benson, P.L., Scales, P.C., Syvertsen, A.K. & Roehlkepartain, E.C. (2012). Is youth spiritual development a universal developmental process? An international exploration. *The Journal of Positive Psychology*, 7(6), 453–470. https://doi.org/10.1080/17439760.2012.732102

Carroll-Meehan, C.J., Brie, J., Kerr, L., Nugent-Jones, M., Wills, R. & Wolniakowska-Majewska, Z. (2024). Competing interests and discourse in early childhood pedagogy and practice in the UK. In W. Boyd & S. Garvis (Eds.), *Early childhood pedagogical practices across the world: Selected case studies on the role of teachers for learning and care*. Singapore: Springer.

de Souza, M. (2010). Meaning and connectedness: Australian perspectives on education and spirituality – An introduction. In M. de Souza & J. Rimes (Eds.), *Meaning and connectedness: Australian perspectives on education and spirituality* (pp. 1–6). Australia: Australian College of Educators.

Eaude, T. (2023). Reflections on the role of spirituality in how young children's identities are constructed. In M.H. Kirmani, A.L. Chapman, B.M. Steele, M. Moallem & S.T. Schroth (Eds.), *Supporting children and youth through spiritual education* (pp. 22–41). Hershey: IGI Global. https://doi.org/10.4018/978-1-6684-6371-0.ch002

Erricker, J. (2009). The importance of happiness to children's education and well-being. In M. de Souza, L.J. Francis, J. O'Higgins-Norman & D. Scott (Eds.), *International handbook of education for spirituality, care and well-being* (pp. 739–752). London & New York: Springer. https://link.springer.com/chapter/10.1007/978-1-4020-9018-9_39

Goodliff, G. (2013). Spirituality expressed in creative learning: Young children's imagining play as space for mediating their spirituality. *Early Child Development and Care*, 183(3), 1054–1071. https://doi.org/10.1080/03004430.2013.792253

Harris, K. (2016). Let's play at the park! Family pathways promoting spiritual resources to inspire nature, pretend play, storytelling, intergenerational play, and celebration. *International Journal of Children's Spirituality*, 21(2), 90–103. https://doi.org/10.1080/1364436X.2016.1164669

Hay, D. & Nye, R. (2006). *The spirit of the child*. London: Jessica Kingsley Publishers.

Hegel, G.W.F. (1977). *Phenomenology of spirit*. London: Clarendon Press.

Hyde, B. (2008). *Children and spirituality: Searching for meaning and connectedness*. London & Philadelphia: Jessica Kingsley Publishers.

Mata-McMahon, J., Haslip, M. & Schein, D. (2019). Early childhood educators' perceptions of nurturing spirituality in secular settings. *Early Child Development and Care*, 189(14), 2233–2251. https://doi.org/10.1080/03004430.2018.1445734

Mata-McMahon, J. & Escarfuller, P. (2023). *Children's spirituality in early childhood education*. New York: Routledge. https://doi.org/10.4324/9781003081463

McCreery, E. (1996). Talking to young people about things spiritual. In R. Best (Ed.), *Education, spirituality and the whole child* (pp. 196–205). London: Cassell.

Mountain, V. (2007). Educational contexts for the development of children's spirituality: Exploring the use of imagination. *International Journal of Children's Spirituality*, 12(2), 191–205. https://doi.org/10.1080/13644360701467535

Pramling Samuelsson, I. (2011). Why we should begin early with ESD: The role of early childhood education. *International Journal of Early Childhood*, 43, 103–118. https://doi.org/10.1007/s13158-011-0034-x

Tang, F. (2022). Nurturing children's spiritual development in early childhood context. *Tapestry*. https://eyfs.info/articles.html/personal-social-and-emotional-development/nurturing-children%E2%80%99s-spiritual-development-in-early-childhood-context-r403/ accessed 12.01.24

Webster, S.R. (2004). An existential framework of spirituality. *International Journal of Children's Spirituality*, 9(1), 7–19. https://doi.org/10.1080/1364436042000200799

1 Children's spirituality, nature and Early Childhood policy

Introduction

The premise of this book is to consider how learning outdoors might inspire a dimension of engagement beyond the immediacy of formal learning, tests and targets, for enhanced well-being and a greater capacity to take responsibility for the well-being of others and the world. Whilst the policy documents for Early Childhood Education from a range of countries globally allude to the attributes of children's spirituality introduced above, whether intentionally or implicitly, it is important to acknowledge and develop an understanding of what this means for the practitioner amid the many and various tasks that must be undertaken in providing high-quality learning experiences for all children. At the outset, this chapter provides an overview of the place of both spirituality and outdoor learning in a selection of countries across the globe. The context of England, from which I write, forms the starting point; however, similarities and differences with other countries' policies will be highlighted, to provide a foundation from which the discussion will then proceed.

Spiritual deficit in policy: United Kingdom

It is widely acknowledged that spirituality is a nebulous concept (Chatterjee, 1989; Adams et al., 2016; Mata-McMahon & Escarfuller, 2023). There is not one definition or meaning, and according to the geographical or historical context, there will be a range of meanings. However, since its inclusion in the *Education Reform Act* (HMSO, 1988), spirituality has continually been a part of educational rhetoric in England. Additionally, since 1992, the National Curriculum in England has stated that schools are required to provide for the Spiritual, Moral, Social, and Cultural (SMSC) development of children. The current *National Curriculum in England* (DfE, 2014), promotes the idea that through the inclusion of spiritual, moral, cultural, mental and physical development of pupils within all aspects of teaching, learning and the wider school experience, children will be prepared for the experiences and opportunities of later life, but equally will develop skills, beliefs and values that will enable them to become responsible members of society (Eaude, 2008).

DOI: 10.4324/9781003483939-2

The requirements for each aspect of SMSC are detailed within the *School Inspection Handbook* (Ofsted, 2022), meaning that all schools are expected to evidence provision for such development. Under the heading 'Spiritual Development' the inspection framework promotes the following as key categories:

- Ability to be reflective about their own beliefs (religious or otherwise) and perspective on life
- Knowledge of, and respect for, different people's faiths, feelings and values
- Sense of enjoyment and fascination in learning about themselves, others and the world around them
- Use of imagination and creativity in their learning
- Willingness to reflect on their experiences

A number of these aspects reflect the hallmarks of spirituality already illustrated through the vignettes, and whilst concern for others' beliefs and faith has not yet been explicitly described, it might be argued that within children's outdoor experiences, respect for the feelings and perspectives of others, including those with special needs and disabilities, was evidenced through their active play. Furthermore, as suggested in the preamble, and as the final bullet point here indicates, the act of reflection on experience is a significant factor in spiritual development. Whilst it concerns the children's personal lives and experiences as expressions of their existence within the world, this is the starting point upon which they can reflect on their own selves as well as their relationship with others in the world to make meaning, then made manifest in action.

It is important to note that the *National Curriculum in England* (DfE, 2014) is statutory for children in Key Stages One and above in England, that is, for children over the age of five. Compulsory schooling begins at this age, before which provision for children from birth to age three is available as childcare and from ages three to five as education. Whilst the experiences of children in early years classes can be seen to illustrate the hallmarks of spirituality as outlined in the *School Inspection Handbook* (Ofsted, 2022), in the context of Early Childhood policy in England, that is, the *Early Years Foundation Stage Statutory Framework* (DfE, 2023) specifically, the word 'spirituality' is absent. This is surprising given the holistic nature of Early Childhood Education, not least due to the influence of early pioneers such as Montessori and Steiner who considered spirituality as the force behind authentic learning (Boyd, 2018).

Goodliff (2016) equates this deficit to the misrepresentation of spirituality as a predominantly religious phenomenon, meaning that there is a danger that the explicit use of the language of spirituality might become problematised by practitioners. Whilst noting that educational policy in England aims to be inclusive, and advising that spirituality and religion are *not* synonymous, Adams et al. (2016) suggest that due to a lack of an agreed definition, there is yet less understanding of what spirituality means in the educational context. Furthermore, Tang and Zhao (2023) note that because of this lack of understanding, there follows a lack of confidence amongst Early Childhood practitioners in supporting young children's spirituality in their settings.

Additionally, Goodliff (2016) cites the influence of the more performative discourse on Early Childhood educational approaches as resulting in the minimisation of the language of spirituality. In their chapter on pedagogical practices in England, Carroll-Meehan et al. (2024) observe that the play-based pedagogy that has historically underpinned Early Childhood Education has been problematised in recent years, in no small way due to the disappointing performance rankings on league tables such as the Programme for International Assessment (PISA). Accordingly, pedagogy has become more formal, driven by targets for outcomes especially in literacy and numeracy, and within the first year of school. Although education in Reception class (ages four to five) is framed by the more holistic *Early Years Foundation Stage Statutory Framework* (DfE, 2023), children now should engage in daily phonics sessions, take part in individual and shared reading, and undertake learning within a curriculum that indicates progression towards the next year and the more performative Key Stage One period of school life. 'School readiness' is also now a feature of the educational rhetoric of the three to five age phase, meaning that an outcomes-based approach to provision, measured against Early Learning Goals, is now the priority for teachers and other practitioners (Carroll-Meehan et al., 2024).

However, whilst teachers in England are expected to direct children's learning according to more narrow guidelines to provide for increased academic success, the hallmarks of spirituality outlined above are at least *implicitly* present within the four principles for practice set out in the *Early Years Foundation Stage statutory framework* (DfE, 2023). For example, 'The Unique Child' concerns a child's holistic development, including good health, creativity, and criticality, and in 'Enabling Environments,' outdoor and open-ended learning is prioritised. Similarly, within one of the key learning areas: 'Understanding the world,' a child's relationship with others and the natural world is encouraged, whilst another: 'Learning and Development' includes playing, exploring, active learning, thinking critically and thinking creatively. Additionally, according to the *School Inspection Handbook* (Ofsted, 2022, p. 334), in relation to Early Childhood Education, an assessment of 'children's personal, social and emotional development is included in routine inspections, including assessors ascertaining whether learners feel safe and are secure, stimulated and happy.'

Much of the above is resonant with spiritual development, again illustrated in the vignettes; yet such aspects of learning might also be considered as part of an existential dimension of education which exists in addition to the personal and social, over and above the performative elements of the curriculum (Wills, 2020). Recognising the importance of this is essential for children in their formative years of learning. When the opportunity to explore a sense of self through creativity, critical thinking and risk-taking is provided, and this sense of self in relation to others is developed through collaboration, listening and sharing in the early years' classroom, it might be argued that as they progress through school, children can draw on these experiences as building blocks to inspire them to become partners in the learning process. Offering a recognition of spirituality within policy and practice would enhance this approach, so to enrich the children's experiences of learning and provide opportunities such as those illustrated earlier.

Aside from spirituality, an encouraging factor within English Early Childhood Education is that exploring the outdoor space is considered significant in young children's learning and development. As a requirement of the *Early Years Foundation Stage Statutory Framework* (DfE, 2023), most settings provide access to an outdoor space at all times of the day. Furthermore, within *Birth to 5 Matters* (Early Education, 2021), non-statutory guidance for the Early Years Foundation Stage, the word 'outdoors' is featured 107 times; this document focuses on the importance of the outdoor space in promoting well-being and inclusion, physical development, relationship building, a chance to relax, and to reflect and make sense of the world. Moreover, akin to the notion of 'biophilia' (Wilson, 1984), *Birth to 5 Matters* emphasises how engagement with nature can promote a sense of responsibility, leading to children becoming 'confident caretakers and problem-solvers of the future' (Early Education, 2021, p. 35). To that end, Tang and Zhao (2023) suggest that spiritual development and outdoor learning should be considered as partners, since the consideration of a dimension beyond the self encourages children to gain an understanding of the wider impact of their attitudes and behaviour on other people as well as the world itself. Resonant of the premise of this book, this idea will be unpacked in more detail in due course.

In concluding this sub-section, it is important to note that due to the political devolution established during the past two decades, each of the four nations of the United Kingdom has articulated their Early Childhood Education policies discretely, therefore prioritising aspects relevant to each cultural context. Along with England, Scotland and Northern Ireland's policies represent a more implicit position regarding the role of spirituality, whereas for children in Wales, a more explicit approach is evident (Goodliff, 2013). 'Moral and Spiritual Development' exists alongside 'Well-being' as a strand within *Curriculum for Wales* (Welsh Government, 2020), which includes children aged three to seven. The skills involved in such development include asking questions, thinking intuitively and creatively, reflecting on ideas, feelings and choices, and developing respect. Therefore, as the discussion continues, it will become clearer how the inclusion of the language of spirituality, not only in England but other contexts, might contribute to the ongoing dynamic and more personal aspect of learning. However, the focus now turns to wider global situations which again evidence a spiritual deficit in policy and practice.

Spiritual deficit in policy: USA, China, Hong Kong and wider

Issues concerning the misrepresentation of spirituality and the performative paradigm of education as stated in relation to English policy are likewise reflected in other contexts. In relation to the USA, Mata-McMahon and Escarfuller (2023) describe how Early Childhood Education in recent years has moved away from a hands-on, sensory approach, which includes the promotion of critical thinking and child-led learning, to one which is now focused on teaching knowledge and skills, assessed through formalised testing.

The authors (McMahon & Escarfuller, 2023) suggest that the shift in perspective concerning Early Childhood Education has meant that schooling has become a means to an end, preparing learners for the world of work, which in turn impacts society economically. Yet they argue, through this approach, children lose out on developing a strong moral compass with an understanding of 'their particular purpose of being' (Mata-McMahon & Escarfuller, 2023, p. 127). They also similarly consider the division of church and state in the USA as problematic for spiritual education. As the advancement of religious beliefs is prohibited in public schools, the promotion of spiritual values is similarly ruled out. Yet there is no clear foundation of understanding of what spirituality might entail as a broader phenomenon outside of a religious context. The authors suggest that spirituality, as an integral aspect of humanity which includes free thinking and creativity as well as 'heart and soul' (Palmer, 2002, cited in Mata-McMahon & Escarfuller, 2023, p. 128), has a place in all sectors of education and that the separation of church and state as it currently exists might provide an opportunity for spirituality to have a place in Early Childhood Education. However, until this understanding becomes widespread, they question how this might happen within the current paradigm and ask teachers to consider a way forward.

In China, Early Childhood policy and practice is similarly sceptical about spirituality. Whilst acknowledging this as an important dimension of the holistic development of young children, according to Zhang (2012), it remains a forgotten area in education. This is due in part, again, to the lack of definition and the absence of a coherent understanding across disciplinary areas such as education, psychology, sociology, religion and theology (Sokanovic & Muller, 1999). In addition to this, the focus from the Ministry of Education (2023) on the development of knowledge and skills, within a paradigm that places great importance on quality and achievement, minimises the amount of time and space given to the more personal dimension of learning. Tang and Zhao (2023, p. 374) suggest that this limits the opportunity for children to engage with aspects of lived experience such as feelings, wondering, confusions and 'the unknown aspects of their lives.' They assert that through spiritual development, the opportunity is available for learners to cultivate behaviours such as inclusivity and self-confidence and thus, they argue that safe spaces, both physical and conceptual, must be created in learning environments to encourage children to 'be healthy in mind, body and spirit and thus contribute to society' (374).

Tang and Zhao (2023) also point out that spiritual development is not a new concept in China, although it is mostly implicit in Early Childhood pedagogy. Nevertheless, whilst spirituality is minimised within practice, it *is* however acknowledged in Early Childhood theory, meaning that it is indeed present within the foundational principles for young children's education. For example, the theories of Early Childhood pioneers such as Friedrich Froebel and Johann Pestalozzi, both of which have a spiritual dimension, are popular and frequently discussed. Also, the educational premise of Heqin Chen (2012), whose ideas form a key underpinning for Early Childhood Education, concerns spirituality not as a religious domain but as a dimension that includes children's emotions, confidence and morality. The premise within *Living Education* (Chen, 2012) is that learning is most effective when children's hearts, emotions, thoughts and consciousness become active. This again promotes a dimension reminiscent of children's spirituality, yet this is still absent from policy.

Similarly, concerning Hong Kong, Ng and Fisher (2022) point out that from the acceptance of the document *A World Fit for Children* (2002, cited in Ng & Fisher, 2022) which was annexed to the resolution of the time, promoting spiritual development as part of a strategy for holistic development became a national priority in the early part of this century. Part of the strategy involved the enhancement of policies and programmes to ensure this development would be implemented. According to Lau (2010), this involved the opportunity for spiritual education including a search for meaning through imagination, creativity and self-expression amongst other values, to form part of a paradigm shift from a technocratic and teacher-centred Early Childhood pedagogy to one that is more child-centred. However, as both Ng and Fisher (2022) and Lau (2010) identify, whilst aspects of holistic development such as the physical, social and emotional are clearly understood by Early Childhood actors, currently the spiritual remains elusive. The authors attribute this deficit to the subjective nature of spirituality, which they suggest has 'multiple meanings' (Ng & Fisher, 2022, p. 142). Furthermore, it is also acknowledged in Hong Kong, as Lau (2010) suggests, that spiritual education is made synonymous with religious education. Focused on a Judeo-Christian or Catholic view of 'God' accepted in schooling during and since the era of British rule, this religious position not only assumes a view of God irrelevant to many children but also prioritises a top-down approach to spiritual education in which a predetermined view of God is presented.

This position is reflected in other countries globally; according to Polemikou and Da Silva (2020, p. 319), policy makers in settings such as Malta, Belgium, Greece and Ireland 'continue to equate spiritual with religious education.' Furthermore Ng and Fisher (2022) note that several OECD (Organisation for Economic Co-Operation and Development) countries (that are mainly European) such as France, Germany, Sweden and Mexico, evidence no explicit mention of spirituality, even within holistic development; and whilst it might be implicit, this is 'not readily found' (Ng & Fisher, 2022, p. 142).

Again, aligned with the premise of this book, the confusion, lack of understanding, and scepticism concerning the language of spirituality might be re-addressed going forward through outdoor learning. It is my conjecture that when experiencing nature and taking part in open-ended activities such as those described in the Preamble, the hallmarks of spirituality become evident – not as religious belief or practice – but as distinct positive human characteristics that promote not only self-awareness and efficacy but a sense of responsibility towards others. This will be unpacked in more detail in due course.

On a more encouraging note, Ng and Fisher (2022) list countries where the spiritual is aligned with holistic development in policy, with Argentina, Tanzania, Norway and Pakistan as examples. They also note that for other contexts, including Australia, New Zealand and Canada, there is an explicit focus on spiritual development within Early Learning goals. This more positive approach is explored now.

Spiritually inclusive policy: Australia and New Zealand

In Australia, a holistic approach to Early Childhood Education is promoted within *Belonging, Being and Becoming: The Early Years Learning Framework for Australia* [EYLF] (Australian Government Department of Education, 2022). In version 2.0., which succeeds the initial document published in 2009 (DEEWR, 2009), the language of spirituality is explicitly used in relation to the holistic, integrated and interconnected approaches presented within. In the Glossary of Terms, 'Spiritual' refers to 'a range of human experiences including a sense of awe and wonder, or peacefulness, and an exploration of being and knowing' (Australian Government Department of Education, 2022, p. 68). Throughout the policy, the term is included within an understanding of pedagogy and learning, respect for diversity, as well as culture and history.

Additionally, spiritual well-being is listed alongside other attributes such as physical, personal, emotional and social development, all of which underpin embodied learning, vital in encouraging children's voice, agency, relationships and responsibility. This underpinning is reminiscent of the hallmarks of spirituality already highlighted such as identity and connectedness, encouraging educators to recognise that such an understanding contributes to 'children's engagement and achievement in learning, development and wellbeing'

(Australian Government Department of Education, 2022, p. 20). Moreover, spirituality is incorporated within an exploration of the significance of the learning environment, including natural spaces for play, discovery and connection. As such, through open-ended interactions within the outdoor space, it is assumed that an appreciation of nature opens the possibility of sustainable behaviour and action.

This policy document, according to Robinson (2019, p. 339), mandates educators working with children aged from birth to five years to 'attend to children's spirituality as a component of their holistic development.' As Adams et al. (2016) point out, the importance placed on connectedness and belonging reveals an intentional creation of a space for spirituality in the classroom and wider school experience. Within this, *Belonging, Being and Becoming* (Australian Government Department of Education, 2022) exhibits a specific emphasis on play-based learning which places the child in the centre of all meaningful learning experiences and highlights the intentional role played by both educators and children in extending and enriching their learning. Inspired by the United Nations Convention on the Rights of the Child (United Nations, 1989) which recognises children's right to play and be active participants in various matters affecting their lives, its vision is that 'all children engage in learning that promotes confident and creative individuals and successful lifelong learners' (Australian Government Department of Education, 2022, p. 6).

The explicit use of spirituality as a key component of this policy (Australian Government Department of Education, 2022) contrasts with that of England and the contexts listed above. Moreover, the five Learning Outcomes for Early Childhood Education demonstrate an intentionality to develop spirituality in children, over and above performative criteria. They are:

- A strong sense of identity – Outcome 1
- A connection with and contribution to the world – Outcome 2
- A strong sense of well-being – Outcome 3
- A confidence in learning – Outcome 4
- Effective communication – Outcome 5

For example, Outcome 1 includes agency, questioning, relationships, self-worth, care and values. The priority placed on *being* reminds educators to focus on the here and now, so to acknowledge who children are as learners. It also focuses on how children negotiate their being through multiple identities, and how to recognise their value and significance within the physical world and relational world of social networks. Outcome 2 concerns connectedness, which involves friendship and care but also an understanding of difference in terms of culture, as well as an understanding of their own. This objective also moves beyond the immediate to consider connectedness with the world and encourages children's active contributions to the environment. This includes

Children's spirituality, nature and Early Childhood policy   17

caring for nature and developing respectful relationships (Robinson, 2019). Finally, the three pillars of Education for Sustainable Development (Kemp, 2018) are reflected in this outcome, through which environmental, social and economic sustainability are encouraged, with an understanding that through positive and proactive behaviours, children might be transformed in the 'way they interact with others and the environment' (Australian Government Department of Education, 2022, p. 38).

Therefore, it might be considered that as Learning Outcome 1 offers a foundational understanding of the personal (spiritual) qualities that form the *a priori* state out of which education then develops, Outcome 2 demonstrates how this might become manifest in action within and for the world. Further to the EYLF (Australian Government Department of Education, 2022), the website of the CCEI (ChildCare Education Institute, 2024) within Australia further purports that spiritual development in young children can lead to a more socially just world. It suggests that within a spiritual curriculum, educators can encourage children to participate in society in positive ways: they can learn to be aware of qualities such as respect, responsibility, and reverence for self and others, as well as acknowledging differences, developing a love for the earth, and taking action to protect it.

Yet from a critical perspective, both Grajczonek (2012) and Robinson (2019) argue that whilst the inclusion of spirituality, especially in relation to children's experiences in the natural environment, is positive, how educators might promote children's spirituality through nature is not clearly articulated. Therefore, further research and training is required in order to support educators in this vital task so that the dimensions of transformation and responsibility contribute to the outward-looking values and behaviours of developing children. I would add that a more explicit explanation of what is understood in relation to the innate capacity of children for spirituality is needed. Therefore, to address this somewhat, the notions of *being* and potentiality, based on children's prior spiritual experiences and the connectedness that they experience with the world and others to bring about change, are explored in more detail in later chapters.

As spirituality is a significant feature of the culture and history of Aotearoa New Zealand, it thereby is even more explicit within Early Childhood Education policy. First published in 1996 and revised in 2017, *Te Whāriki* is New Zealand's curriculum for Early Childhood and covers the education of children from the time they are born until age five (New Zealand Ministry for Education, 1996, 2017). The Early Learning Curriculum Framework (New Zealand Ministry for Education, 2023) is also currently available. Initially, *Te Whāriki* was created in collaboration between Indigenous and non-Indigenous educators with the intention to embrace a truly multicultural educational experience. According to Sachdev (2016), practitioners are professionally obligated to contribute to the spiritual growth of children in order to honour the Treaty of Waitangi, New Zealand's founding document. The signing of this document in 1840 ensued a commitment on the part of the Māori people and 'Pakeha' to live together 'in a spirit of partnership' (New Zealand Ministry for Education, 2017). Accordingly, the curriculum upholds this principle through a pedagogy which is bicultural, holistic and inclusive.

The main vision of *Te Whāriki* is that students are 'competent and confident learners and communicators, healthy in mind, body and spirit, secure in their sense of belonging and in the knowledge that they make a valued contribution to society' (New Zealand Ministry for Education, 2017, p. 6). As such, spirituality might be considered as one of the central principles of *the curriculum*. Greenfield (2018) observes that the 2017 version of *Te Whāriki* has a strong emphasis on spirituality. This is underlined in the document's acknowledgement that for Māori, the child is a link to the world of the ancestors and to the new world, connected to people, places, things and the spiritual realm (New Zealand Ministry for Education, 2017, p. 52). This is also made explicit within the *Early Learning Curriculum Framework* (New Zealand Ministry for Education, 2023, p. 2) in which the first principle highlights how learners should 'understand their own mana atuatanga – uniqueness and spiritual connectedness.' The corresponding Learning Outcome aims for children 'to keep themselves safe – physically, emotionally, intellectually and spiritually – so that their ancestral mana is upheld.' This is illustrated by Fraser (2004, p. 91) in her representation of a response from a teacher: 'When I talk with a child, about what they are doing, I do not just see that child in front of me. I see all the people connected to that child, going back generations in a great cluster.'

Within this understanding is the notion of well-being; as a result, educators are required to support 'the well-being of the child, along with their sense of self and spirituality' (New Zealand Ministry for Education, 2017, p. 28). Indeed, the revised policy document recognises the 'importance of spirituality in the development of the whole child' (New Zealand Ministry for Education, 2017, p. 30). This document offers a significantly different approach to the *Early Years Foundation Stage* policy of England (DfE, 2023) in its acknowledgement of the significance of the spirit of the child in contributing to well-being. In order to promote such a value, *Te Whāriki* believes that each child is on their own unique journey.

The term 'Te Whāriki' means 'woven mat.' Whilst the upper side of the woven mat displays the weaver's artistry as complete, the underside reveals their mastery within the process of creating. As stated in the curriculum document, the activity of weaving a whāriki takes knowledge, skill and time and, when finished, the intricate handiwork is valued for its artistry (New Zealand Ministry for Education, 2017, p. 10). This image provides a metaphor for the Early Childhood curriculum. In weaving a whāriki, the loose strands that might look incomplete and messy indeed represent the potentiality of children in their learning and personal development. As Bone (2008) notes, the curriculum is holistic, with the whāriki mat representative of strands and principles

Children's spirituality, nature and Early Childhood policy 19

that weave together. This includes the spiritual dimension. As new strands are woven in to expand the existing whāriki mat, children's experiences, which represent new learning, allow educators to listen and observe, so as to encourage young children to develop in their own areas of interest and make contributions to their own learning.

Reminiscent of the philosophies of the Early Childhood pioneers, explored in a later chapter, here, children are valued as active learners with learning almost always collaborative. In reference to 'Mana Tangata,' Early Childhood Education involves all participants working together 'for the common good' to enable the outworking of the principles of respect and reciprocity. It also encourages the involvement of the family (whānau) in the learning process. The curriculum includes events that occur both directly and indirectly in an Early Childhood setting, and children learn through play. They ask questions, interact with others, work out theories, and engage purposefully with resources. It is this exploratory approach that instils positive behaviours and attitudes that will continue to be an influence throughout life. Learning, in partnership with adults and other children, is encouraged so that each might be empowered to thrive within an increasingly diverse yet connected society (New Zealand Ministry for Education, 2017).

The outworking of the philosophy of *Te Whariki* is provided through five strands. Each of the five strands has a name in both English and Māori. While these names are very closely related, different cultural contexts mean they are not equivalents. Along with the principles of *Te Whariki* and the Learning Outcomes, these strands create a framework for a holistic curriculum for Early Childhood. The strands are:

1. Well-being – Mana atua
2. Belonging – Mana whenua
3. Contribution   Mana tangata
4. Communication – Mana reo
5. Exploration – Mana aotūroa

As stated above, spirituality is explicit within the whole curriculum document. However, akin to the Australian Framework (Australian Government Department for Education, 2022), *Te Whariki* draws on the foundational acknowledgement and understanding of an intrinsic spirituality in all learners in order to promote a sense of connectedness with the world and others, leading to inclusive behaviour and taking social responsibility. It is argued here, and will be developed further in due course, that whilst the aspirations stated for children within *Te Whāriki* are in some ways similar to those of the EYFS (DfE, 2023), the curriculum for New Zealand goes much further in promoting learners as becoming secure in their sense of belonging as well as understanding the value of their contributions to society. In outworking this purpose, children will learn to keep themselves safe, care for the world, treat others fairly and learn to work with others (New Zealand Ministry for Education, 2023).

Similar to how the Australian curriculum is open to critique, so is this expression of Early Childhood Education. Tesar (2015) argues that *Te Whariki* is predominantly a philosophy rather than a curriculum. As such, he suggests that as a policy document, it does not provide enough structure or direction, it is highlighted that as a policy document, it does not provide enough structure or direction, and rather than focusing on culture, history and relationships, it would be more effective for teachers if it were more explicitly related to learning goals, with outcomes against which progress might be assessed. Yet, not wanting to align with the performative paradigm prevalent in other countries, Tesar (2015) acknowledges the value of the open-ended approach to learning and therefore suggests the possibility that *Te Whariki* in fact occupies a third space as a curriculum framework that locates itself not as an alternative to a performative approach but one which acknowledges that what has meaning for learners is beyond what they come to understand as fact, and that education, as well as encouraging academic progress, also reflects their own experiences, thoughts, questions and responses.

Concluding comments

To conclude this chapter, it is important to acknowledge that in line with Australia and New Zealand, Canadian Early Childhood policy is also inclusive of the language of spirituality. According to Pytka and Mirkovic (2024), the policy document for early years teaching in Ontario acknowledges the need for educators to recognise the spiritual within children's experiences for their well-being, learning and growth. Interestingly, the understanding of what spirituality means is very much akin to the categories described in the vignettes, to be unpacked further in the next chapter. Hallmarks such as connectedness, imagination, identity and concern for others feature in the policy and activities are suggested to encourage teachers in their practice. Also, whilst it is unclear as to the theoretical framework that underpins the notion of spirituality in English policy for example, Canadian policy and pedagogies are rooted in the literature of scholars actively researching this subject. In the next chapter, what is meant by spirituality will be explored from a theoretical and philosophical perspective. The hallmarks already highlighted will be identified as identities of spirituality (Kirmani & Kirmani, 2009), and attention will be given to how these hallmarks might be made manifest through children's engagement with nature.

Finally, it is interesting to note that contexts in which the language of spirituality is explicit are those with rich Indigenous communities, many of whom have a strong relationship to the spiritual through history and connections with the natural environment. Further attention will be given to this in due course. However it should be considered at this point that since spirituality here is explored largely from a Western academic perspective, this can only provide a partial understanding of what it means for young children in a range of non-Western communities. Therefore, the limitations of this discussion are acknowledged, and in a later chapter, the issue of decolonisation in Early Childhood Education will be addressed.

References

Adams, K., Bull, L. & Maynes, M.L. (2016). Towards an understanding of the distinctive features of young children's spirituality. *European Early Childhood Education Research Journal*, 24(5), 760–774. https://doi.org/10.1080/1350293X.2014.996425

Australian Government Department of Education. (2022). *Belonging, being and becoming: The early years learning framework for Australia* [EYLF] -(V2.0). ACT: Australian Government Department of Education for the Ministerial Council. Available from: https://www.acecqa.gov.au/sites/default/files/2023-01/EYLF-2022-V2.0.pdf

Bone, J. (2008). Exploring trauma, loss and healing: Spirituality, *Te Whāriki* and early childhood education. *International Journal of Children's Spirituality*, 13(3), 265–276. https://doi.org/10.1080/13644360802236532

Boyd, D. (2018). Early childhood education for sustainability and the legacies of two pioneering giants. *Early Years*, 38(2), 227–239. https://doi.org/10.1080/09575146.2018.1442422

Carroll-Meehan, C.J., Brie, J., Kerr, L., Nugent-Jones, M., Wills, R. & Wolniakowska-Majewska, Z. (2024). Competing interests and discourse in early childhood pedagogy and practice in the UK. In W. Boyd & S. Garvis (Eds.), *Early childhood pedagogical practices across the world: Selected case studies on the role of teachers for learning and care*. Singapore: Springer.

Chatterjee, M. (1989). *The concept of spirituality*. Columbia: South Asia Books.

Chen, H.Q. (2012). *Living education*. Nanjing: Nanjing Normal University Press.

ChildCare Education Institute. (2024). *Pinnacle curriculum*. Available from: cceionline.com

Department for Education. (2014). *National curriculum in England*. Available from: https://www.gov.uk/government/publications/national-curriculum-in-england-framework-for-key-stages-1-to-4

Department for Education. (2023). *Early years foundation stage statutory framework*. Available from: https://assets.publishing.service.gov.uk/media/65aa5e42ed27ca001327b2c7/EYFS_statutory_framework_for_group_and_school_based_providers.pdf

Department for Education, Employment and Workplace Relations [DEEWR]. (2009). *Belonging, being and becoming: The early years learning framework for Australia* [EYLF]. Canberra: Commonwealth of Australia. Available from: https://docs.education.gov.au/node/2632

Early Education. (2021). *Birth to 5 matters: Non-statutory guidance for the early years foundation stage*. Available from: https://birthto5matters.org.uk/wpcontent/uploads/2021/04/Birthto5Matters-download.pdf

Eaude, T. (2008). *Children's spiritual, moral, social and cultural development: Primary and early years*. London: Sage.

Fraser, D. (2004). Secular schools, spirituality and Maori values. *Journal of Moral Education*, 33(1), 87–95. https://doi.org/10.1080/1364436990040104

Goodliff, G. (2013). Spirituality expressed in creative learning: Young children's imagining play as space for mediating their spirituality. *Early Child Development and Care*, 183(3), 1054–1071. https://doi.org/10.1080/03004430.2013.792253

Goodliff, G. (2016). Spirituality in early childhood education and care. In M. de Souza, J. Bone & J. Watson (Eds.), *Spirituality across disciplines: Research and practice* (pp. 67–80). Netherlands: Springer. https://doi.org/10.1007/978-3-319-31380-1

Grajczonek, J. (2012). Interrogating the spiritual as constructed in belonging, being and becoming: The early years learning framework for Australia. *Australasian Journal of Early Childhood*, 37(1), 152–160. https://doi.org/10.1177/183693911203700118

Greenfield, C.F. (2018). Investigation into New Zealand early childhood teachers' perspectives on spirituality and wairua in teaching. *International Journal of Children's Spirituality*, 23(3), 275–290. https://doi.org/10.1080/1364436X.2018.1460333

HMSO. (1988). *Education reform act*. London: HMSO.

Kemp, N. (2018). Early childhood education for sustainability. In S. Powell & K. Smith (Eds.), *An introduction to early childhood studies* (pp. 247–259). Los Angeles: Sage.

Kirmani, M.H. & Kirmani, S. (2009). Recognition of seven spiritual identities and its implications on children. *International Journal of Children's Spirituality*, 14(4), 369–383. https://doi.org/10.1080/13644360903293630

Lau, G. (2010). Research on children's concepts of God and spirituality and its implications on educational inequality in early childhood educational reform in Hong Kong. *International Journal of Educational Reform*, 19(4), 224–246. https://doi.org/10.1177/105678791001900401

Mata-McMahon, J. & Escarfuller, P. (2023). *Children's spirituality in early childhood education*. New York: Routledge. https://doi.org/10.4324/9781003081463

Ministry of Education: The People's Republic of China. (2023). Available from: www.moe.gov.cn

New Zealand Ministry for Education. (1996). *Te Whāriki*. Wellington: Ministry of Education. Available from: http://www.educate.ece.govt.nz/learning/curriculumAndLearning/TeWhariki.aspx

New Zealand Ministry for Education. (2017). *Te Whāriki: He Whāriki Mātauranga mō ngā Mokopuna o Aotearoa Early Childhood Curriculum*. Available from: https://www.education.govt.nz/assets/Documents/Early-Childhood/Te-Whariki-Early-Childhood-Curriculum-ENG-Web.pdf

New Zealand Ministry for Education. (2023). *Early learning curriculum framework. He Anga Marau Kohungahunga*. Available from: https://assets.education.govt.nz/public/Documents/News/News-2023/Early-Learning-Curriculum-Framework-2023.pdf

Ng, D.T.K. & Fisher, J.W. (2022). Kindergarten teachers' spiritual well-being impacts holistic early childhood education. *International Journal of Children's Spirituality*, 27(3–4), 141–157. https://doi.org/10.1080/1364436X.2022.2066067

Office for Standards in Education, Children's Services and Skills. (2022). *School inspection handbook*. Available from: https://www.gov.uk/government/publications/school-inspection-handbook-eif/school-inspection-handbook

Polemikou, A. & Da Silva, J.P. (2020). Readressing spiritual growth: What can we learn from childhood education? *Journal of Humanistic Psychology*, 62(3), 334–351. https://doi.org/10.1177/0022167820938612

Pytka, B. & Mirkovic, D. (2024). Children's spirituality: Implications for practice. Available from: https://cccf-fcsge.ca/ece-resources/topics/childhood-development/link-between-spirituality-emotional-well-being-in-children/

Robinson, C. (2019). Young children's spirituality: A focus on engaging with nature. *Australasian Journal of Early Childhood*, 44(4), 339–350. https://doi.org/10.1177/1836939119870907

Sachdev, G. (2016). Spirituality in the early childhood education in New Zealand and around the globe: Relevance, research and beyond. *Practitioner Researcher*, 4(4), 17–23.

Sokanovic, M. & Muller, D. (1999). Professional and educational perspectives on spirituality in young children. *Pastoral Care in Education*, 17(1), 9–16.

Tang, F. & Zhao, J. (2023). Spirituality in early childhood pedagogy: A Froebelian Lens on the role of women in a Chinese context. In T. Bruce, Y. Nishida, S. Powell, H. Wasmuth & J. Winnett (Eds.), *The Bloomsbury handbook to Friedrich Froebel* (pp. 372–380). London: Bloomsbury Publishing.

Tesar, M. (2015). New Zealand perspective on early childhood education: Nāku te rourou nāu te rourou ka ora ai te iwi. *Journal of Pedagogy*, 6(2), 9–18. https://doi.org/10.1515/jped-2015-0010

United Nations. (1989). *Convention on the rights of the child*. London: Unicef.

Welsh Government. (2020). *Curriculum for Wales*. Available from: https://hwb.gov.wales/curriculum-for-wales

Wills, R. (2020). *Learning beyond the objective in primary education: Philosophical perspectives from theory and practice*. Abingdon: Routledge.

Wilson, E.O. (1984). *Biophilia*. Cambridge, Massachusetts and London: Harvard University Press.

Zhang, K. (2012). Spirituality and early childhood special education: Exploring a 'forgotten' dimension. *International Journal of Children's Spirituality*, 17(1), 39–49. https://doi.org/10.1080/1364436X.2012.660475

2 Children's spirituality, nature and frameworks of understanding

Introduction

The notion of children's spirituality has become a focus for conversation over the past three decades. As already stated, the language of spirituality within Early Childhood Education in some countries is explicit within policy for schools and pre-school settings, yet in many others it is neglected or misunderstood. A common misconception is its equivalence with religion; the plurality of meanings partnered with a lack of agreed definition also results in its absence from policy and therefore practice in a range of contexts across the globe. Nevertheless, it is argued here that spirituality *is* evident within children's educational experiences in their early childhood, both as a part of, and aside from religious education; therefore the current discussion advocates for its inclusion in the rhetoric, programmes and policies that cater for the growth and nurture of young children.

In England, its inclusion in the Education Acts of 1944, 1988 and 2002 (Adams et al., 2015) reflects a reticence on the part of the Government and House of Lords to erase this aspect from educational experience. This is in some part due to the continued relationship between church and state within a perceived view of England as a Christian country; nevertheless, it is significant that the language of spirituality has and continues to form an important part of educational policy for children mostly aged over five. Furthermore, in England this language does not specifically relate to religion or religious education.

In 1988 the Education Act stated that schools would satisfy requirements if they were seen to:

> promote the spiritual, moral, cultural, mental and physical development of pupils, and prepare such pupils for the opportunities, responsibilities and experiences of adult life.
>
> (HMSO, 1988, preamble)

Published in 1995, the government-endorsed document Spiritual and Moral Development provided a broad description of spirituality:

something fundamental in the human condition which is not necessarily experienced through the physical senses and/or expressed through everyday language. It has to do with relationships with other people and, for believers, with God. It has to do with the universal search for individual identity ... it is to do with the search for meaning and purpose in life.

(SCAA, 1995, p. 3)

Therefore, it might be suggested that a humanistic view of spirituality is evident here, and whilst not negating or undermining the role of religious belief and practice, it is not essential that children participate in such practices to engage with and express the spiritual dimension of their lived existence.

As a teacher in an English primary school, with a career (including my student and early career teacher years) that spans from 1988 to the present day, due to its inclusion in policy for children aged five and over, spirituality has always been a familiar concept. However, more recently as an academic, I have been curious to locate this understanding within a theoretical and philosophical framework. Put simply, I have asked: 'where does this understanding of spirituality come from?' There is a consensus amongst colleagues (for example as highlighted by Adams et al., 2016) that the theoretical underpinning for the notion of spirituality in the policies included above is vague and that the wider context for understanding spirituality is unclear within statutory documentation. Nevertheless, a burgeoning bank of academic literature from both within the UK and beyond either supports or resonates with the view of spirituality as an innate human phenomenon. Thus, a brief overview of pertinent texts is provided here.

Children's spirituality literature

An early publication on the topic of children's spirituality is *The Spiritual Life of Children* by Robert Coles (1990). Having listened to the remarks of children met during his years as a practitioner in paediatrics and child psychiatry, Coles argues that spirituality is an innate phenomenon and as such, children are spiritual beings. He also believes that spirituality is universal. Having used drawings, paintings and conversations in research to gain extensive evidence of the spiritual lives of children from many countries and traditions, he concludes that the spiritual can be experienced through everyday occurrences. Therefore, both educational environments and activities outside of a religious context, within any culture, can afford spiritual awareness and development in young children. Coles' assertions are supported in the work of zoologist Alister Hardy who maintains that spirituality is biological, therefore innate and universal, and essential to human survival. In *The Spiritual Nature of Man* (1979), Hardy refers to spirituality as a transcendental reality that is encountered by all, and spiritual experience as numinous, where the self can experience unity with the dimension existing beyond the self. Therefore, it might be suggested that spirituality concerns both the inner life of the child whilst also evoking an awareness of something other or beyond.

The first aspect suggested by Coles (1990) – that is the notion of an innate spirituality – implies that as an *a priori* state of being, spirituality provides the starting point for an existential understanding that has an ontological basis. It concerns the primordial dimension of humanity which exists *before* the construction of any systems of knowledge, belief or values and therefore, within an understanding of a child's potentiality, it provides a starting point for how individuals experience the world. In turn, it is a priority in the formation of identity, underpins a sense of belonging in the world, and as an essential factor in learning, influences the ways in which individuals reflect on their experiences to make meaning. Also noted by Mata-McMahon and Escarfuller (2023), a child's 'being' is an essential aspect of their spirituality and this provides the starting point from which they can reflect on their lived experience, including their selves and the world around them, in order to construct meaning.

This is illustrated further by David Hay and Rebecca Nye who in *The Spirit of the Child* (2006), refer to 'being' as the starting point of learning. Expressed as 'relational consciousness,' spirituality here is understood as an innate phenomenon that includes an ontological connectedness with others. 'Others' are cited as the world, people, self and God. As each child's being inspires learning in relation to each context of other, meaning and truth become not just objective perspectives but emerge through the awareness of a 'new dimension of understanding, meaning and experience' (2006, p. 109). Hay and Nye also conclude from their research that spirituality is a vital aspect of lived reality. They identify 'relational consciousness' as 'an unusual plane of consciousness or perceptiveness' (109) that allows individuals to gain a heightened awareness of their own spiritual existence.

From a philosophical perspective, the ideas offered here have resonance with the thoughts of Martin Heidegger whose writings provide a wider framework for exploration. Heidegger (1962) describes the *a priori* dimension noted here as spirituality as pertaining to the starting point of all human experience: the basic state of Being-in-the-world. The notion of 'world' here is not presented as a particular realm but as the open-ness of Being, with 'Being' not precisely *a* being but an open question of Being (Heidegger, 1978). Within this open-ness, a conceptual space, Being allows for the possibility of unity with others in the world. But significantly founded on an ontological understanding of Being, it is the possibility of Being (*Dasein*), rather than form and function, that is made manifest through the 'connectedness of life' (Heidegger, 1962, pp. 426–427).

From this state of Being, authentic learning, which includes the movement of *Dasein* into its own potentiality-for-Being, might be inspired. As existentially interconnected, Being and learning cannot be separated. Therefore rather than being projected into fixed ideas or truths that subsequently become foundational within systems and schemes defined by language and culture, or what Heidegger calls a representational positing of the world (Heidegger, 1978), educators for spirituality are encouraged to consider what comes 'before' representation and allow this to be brought forth into consciousness. Tubbs writes: 'teaching calls for this: to let learn' (2005, p. 131); in this, the educator allows the children to learn learning itself (132). As it unfolds into its own potentiality, *Dasein* becomes the possibility for spiritual awareness, ontological connectedness and personal meaning-making (Heidegger, 1962).

Within the discipline of children's spirituality, a number of authors expand on this view in their published work. Hay and Nye, as suggested above, consider a perceptive rather than cognitive understanding of spirituality. They describe a reflexive process whereby one is not fully conscious of an event or person but is 'aware of one's awareness' (2006, p. 65). This is identified as having importance in spiritual practice where the self, apprehended within a primordial consciousness, becomes aware of different contexts of other. Categories of awareness sensing resonate with the illustrations provided in the vignettes outlined in the Preamble, and for the authors (Hay & Nye, 2006), these categories highlight where a child is *aware* of a sense of something other in a special moment. They might become aware of corporeality and the bodily 'felt sense' of an activity (2006, p. 70), aware of empathy or belonging (68), and aware of a connection with his or her surroundings (66). Awareness is not knowledge. It is rather a holistic 'sense' or feeling in which one resonates with another and has no need for articulation or definition.

Spirituality, as an open-ended response to one's *Dasein* (Heidegger, 1962) allows for meaning to be made without the influence of an overarching metanarrative. As Gelven (1970) points out, this is a process of ontological enquiry validated by its location within the self and its reflection on itself as truth in its existence (1970, p. 24). Hart (2003) adopts a similar view. For him, the whole of life is a spiritual event – an ongoing responsiveness to possibility inspiring liberation, transformation, enlightenment and self-realisation (Hart, 2003, pp. 9–10). The end result is not pre-ordained and authority lies within the self. Truth is organic as it unfolds throughout life (9). This notion of course is open to critique, and in due course will be unpacked from a more critical perspective; yet it is important to note that in promoting a humanistic view of spirituality, separated but not necessarily divorced from religion, many authors prioritise the learner's own self as the locus of authentic learning.

The view of ontology as the platform for possibility is shared by other spiritual educators and academics (de Souza et al., 2004; Hyde, 2008), most of whom still have influence within the field in 2024. A number are concerned with a holistic approach to education that reflects a connectedness with the world and others (e.g. Miller, 2000; Tacey, 2004; Adams et al., 2008) whilst further scholars consider the affective dimension of human experience which is over and above cognisable understanding (e.g. Hart, 2003; Hay &

Nye, 2006; de Souza, 2010). Akin to Heidegger's idea of the open-ness of Being (1978), Scott (2001) suggests that the significance of spirituality is that it requires an open space for 'voicing lived experience which is not dependent on external evidence or objective detail' (2001, p. 120). As such, Scott encourages the educator in developing this ontological awareness to open a conceptual space for engagement and to be willing to 'attend to something in its own right.' As Heidegger succinctly puts it the teacher must allow the self to 'let it be' (1978, p. 220).

As already noted, spirituality concerns both inner expressions of 'being' but also responses to the natural world and even the dimension beyond the immediate. An early description of spirituality offered by Elaine McCreery (1996, p. 197) states that spirituality is 'an awareness that there is something other, something greater than the course of everyday events.' Elaine Champagne (2001) focuses on mystery, presence and wonder as ways in which children rest in the moment of their Being; furthermore, both Schein (2018) and Keltner (2023) write about experiences of awe as the inspiration for the development of joy, leading to a greater sense of community and creativity, and resulting in personal transformation and empathy for others.

In many ways, as is the subject of this book, children's outdoor experiences provide the starting point for such spiritual expressions. As Hay and Nye (2006) indicate, an awareness of awe and wonder in seeing a waterfall or sunset, for example, is characteristic of an aesthetic appreciation of nature that might inspire mystery and contemplation. They also write that a sense of awe might be awakened by more innocuous events such as 'a flame appearing when a match is struck or a light being switched on, or water coming out of a tap' (2006, p. 72). Nevertheless, being beyond language and logic, again it is the *a priori* state of Being-in-the-world (Heidegger, 1962) which allows for the personal response to nature that can in turn inspire a connection with the numinous. This is an organic pedagogical process. Transmission of information is evaded, yet a transcendent dimension, which cannot be taught, as Rudolph Otto argues, is 'awakened by the spirit' (1950, p. 60).

Reflecting on her educational practice within the Early Childhood sector, Schein (2018) identifies how aspects of spirituality such as connectivity, enquiry and wonder, as well as transcendence, become manifest within children's outdoor learning experiences. As the inspiration for reflection and critical thinking, young children, when active in nature, can respond naturally to themselves and others in a way that is less restricted, drawing on imagination and creativity, and allowing for risk and adventure. Her own perspective on spiritual development provides a framework within which educators might nurture spirituality from the humanistic perspective outlined here. This includes having meaningful purpose, the opportunity to develop an individual character and a reason to care for other living things. She also purports that 'love, connections and relationships lead to a positive sense of self' (Schein, 2018, p. 135) and suggests that parents and educators offer opportunities for the spiritual development of young children in nature, both at home and in the public space.

Also working in the Early Childhood sector, Mata-McMahon and Escarfuller (2023) similarly suggest that spirituality equates to holistic development, with a focus on meaning and connectedness; they also consider that spirituality provides the opportunity for children to 'bear witness to truths learned about life,' to 'tell their stories' and to ask 'ultimate questions' (2023, p. 21). Additionally they suggest that spirituality might again be exercised through play, again providing opportunities for children to experience moments of wonder, awe, joy and inner-peace. These ideas resonate with Hart (2003) who identifies spirituality in terms of: moments of wonder, finding inner wisdom, asking big questions about meaning and life, expressing compassion and seeing beneath the surface of the material world. Hart names these 'touchstones' for young children's spiritual lives. Again, experiences in nature can be the inspiration for the development of these touchstones.

Through this discussion so far, it has been intimated several times how young children's experiences in nature can become the starting point for spiritual awareness and development. Robinson (2020) explores this from an Early Childhood perspective within the context of Australia. As noted in the previous chapter, the Australian mandatory *Early Years Learning Framework* (DEEWR, 2009; Australian Government Department of Education, 2022) 'outlines pedagogical principles, practices and learning outcomes to assist educators in attending to children's holistic development, including their spirituality' (Robinson, 2020, pp. 254–255). However, Robinson argues that for effective spiritual development, educators must possess the skills to be able to identify spiritual moments in children's play and active learning, and as noted in Chapter One, should be able to implement in practice the suggestions for spiritual development as stated in the policy. She provides a number of themes that, drawn from educator's understandings and practices offered within research data, indicate how the spiritual might be 'afforded' in the classroom. These include connectedness to people and nature, play, social and social-skill development and conversation.

As an 'affordance,' connectedness to people and nature is the concern of the discussion going forward. According to Hyde (2022), Gibson's affordance theory (2015, cited in Hyde, 2022), which suggests the value and significance that environments and objects have to an individual, can be applied to outdoor spaces. Hyde suggests, drawing on Warden (2018, cited in Hyde, 2022), that outdoor spaces afford a plethora of opportunities for children to play and explore, for inventiveness and the development of inter-connected relationships. Again, when the pedagogical process has an ontological basis, it is the child's 'being' that provides the starting point for spiritual awareness; in relation to nature as an affordance, the conceptual space within which personal learning takes place (Heidegger, 1962; Scott, 2001), allows for the opportunity for the identification and nurture of the various hallmarks of spirituality identified so far.

Spiritual identities

From this ontological starting point, it is now necessary to provide a framework for how children's experiences in nature afford the development of spirituality in Early Childhood Education. In this chapter, I draw on seven spiritual identities as highlighted by Kirmani and Kirmani (2009), and the spiritual characteristics of an emergent curriculum for early years children proposed by Farrugia and Gellel (2022). Emerging from the authors' qualitative research into understandings of spirituality amongst participants across a range of religious groups, areas of academic interest and ages, Kirmani and Kirmani (2009) identify seven spiritual identities, four of which have relevance to the current discussion. In the framework of spiritual development proposed by Farrugia and Gellel (2022), ten characteristics of spirituality as derived from existing literature are posited as having resonance, reflecting the pedagogy of Loris Malaguzzi, founder of the Reggio Emilia approach to Early Childhood Education, and particularly the notion of the child as a capable learner being nurtured through positive relationships within a community of learners in environments that are both challenging and joyous (Stremmel, 2012 cited in Farrugia & Gellel, 2022). Whilst the framework for understanding spirituality drawn from the research of Kirmani and Kirmani (2009) was based on responses from participants of different ages, the framework offered by Farrugia and Gellel (2022) is located specifically within the paradigm of Early Childhood Education and Care.

In their research, Kirmani and Kirmani (2009) first identify a *Sensocentric* spiritual sensitivity. This concerns participants 'centring on auditory, visual, and tactile senses' (Kirmani & Kirmani, 2009, p. 374), for example, hearing birds chirping or the feel of wind on the face. This identity might be further inspired by multi-sensory activities such as finger painting and listening to music, but the authors suggest that in relation to children's experiences of nature, allowing them to have free play and access to plants, flowers and trees, as well as natural objects and sounds, teachers can promote reflection on this sensory experience of the outdoor environment. Practically, engaging with the sights, sounds, smells and textures of the outdoor space creates a rich and immersive experience for young children. Similarly, Robinson (2019), writing from an Australian context, identifies how Indigenous peoples place importance on the natural environment as a component of their identity and sense of belonging.

Schein (2018) concurs with the notion of a sensory spiritual sensitivity, but also highlights how nature might be brought into the indoor space through teachers allowing children to handle rocks, sticks, shells and leaves in the classroom. In recognition of the barriers to nature that exist, societally, socially and economically (Louv, 2005), it is important to explore how practitioners might develop sensory spiritual awareness within their given environments and constraints whilst at the same time exposing them to the opportunity afforded by natural matter (Hyde, 2022). Therefore, it might be suggested that an understanding of children's spiritual awareness might encourage practitioners to consider natural places and objects as affordances for the Senso-centric aspect of spirituality, to act as a window into their inner world, and allow them to express their inner thoughts and feelings beyond the physical and immediate.

The second spiritual sensitivity identified by Kirmani and Kirmani (2009), the *Socio-centric,* involves the interactions and relationships between the self and others, be they other people or other living things. This resonates with Miller's (2015) idea that for young children, all aspects of nature, as an extension of themselves, are to be cared for. She notes this as both an innately human and innately spiritual concern. Accordingly, she notes, children will naturally respond to animals and trees with a sense of responsibility and will want to communicate with nature in an empathetic way. This might include a desire to protect the earth or become involved in renewable activity for the future. She continues that 'children identify deeply with animals' (Miller, 2015, p. 126) and that 'children find in them an embodied vocabulary for their own emotions and energies' (127). Care for animals notably, can become a healing force, particularly for children who have not experienced unconditional love, and for those whose relationships are broken.

This is illustrated through the initial visit of the guinea pig to the youngest children in my school. During this visit, the children expressed their care for the pet by stroking him and talking to him, giving him carrots to eat and making sure he had enough water. Following this, the children's interest was piqued. As a result, further learning on how to care for animals was introduced in the classroom, and children were encouraged to look at books and videos about small animals. During the second visit, the children expressed their care for the guinea pig by asking if they could create a small area for him to relax in the outdoor space; they also wanted him to be active, so they developed a small obstacle course similar to those created in their own physical play, and finally they introduced a feeding and drinking point so he could be refreshed. For the children with Special Educational Needs and Disabilities, the connection with the guinea pig was strong. They were able to communicate non-verbally with meaning and affection, and as the animal seemed to reciprocate this affection, the sense of joy was visible on their faces and through their body language. Caring for animals is an excellent means for developing a sense of identity and self-efficacy, even in the early years of a child's life. As Miller states: nature 'helps us see the larger picture, our place in it, and our place in relation to other things' (2015, p. 128).

Kirmani and Kirmani (2009) suggest that this also extends to inclusion and diversity, to 'develop a sense of belongingness' and acceptance of difference. In turn, social behaviours are effected, often in positive ways; for example, 'working for social justice' was highlighted as important in their research data, as was a sense of helping others in the community (2009, p. 374), as well as a desire to do 'service to humanity.' This is underlined by Mata-McMahon and Escarfuller (2023), who suggest that spirituality provides evidence for the importance of friendship and close relationships during the early years, and argue that through play and relationality, young children's friendships offer an opportunity to experience interconnectedness. In this respect, a child's sense of self and relationship with others can lead to a sense of responsibility for others, locally or globally (Adams et al., 2008), reflected in Schein's proposition (2018) that, from the basis of experiencing care and kindness, children will respond in acts of care and kindness.

The *Eco-centric* sensitivity proposed by Kirmani and Kirmani (2009) is named through words such as harmony, connection and peace. A sense of the power and complexity of nature is also highlighted, with spirituality in this context often being an individual rather than a collective experience. The relationship between the self and the world is a continuing theme within the discourse of children's spirituality. Robinson (2019), for example describes spirituality as possessing an awareness of self in relation to the local and natural environment, and other authors such as Adams et al. (2008) assert that experiences of, for example, walking in the countryside, not only instil 'a sense of beauty and freedom' (2008, p. 115) but enable children to 'gain a sense of being part of something greater than themselves' (116). This reinforces the assertion of Bone et al. (2007) that spirituality connects people to nature, all living things and the universe, and thus inspires a sense of wonder and mystery even within daily life.

Again relating this to the Indigenous experience of nature, whilst we often consider the Self-World relation (Hay & Nye, 2006) as ontological and therefore essential to children's spiritual development, it is important to note that within some cultures, there is no division between human life and other forms of life in the natural world (Lee-Hammond, 2017, cited in Robinson, 2019), and that such a dualism might for some children run counter to their own understanding and experiences. This is underlined by Gergen (2009) and in my own writing (Wills, 2012), with both texts suggesting that ontologically it is difficult for some to accept that there are borders between self and any category of other (Buber, 1970). In this respect, spirituality within Early Childhood Education must adopt culturally appropriate experiences and attitudes, whilst recognising how learners might become aware of their own spiritual awareness.

It is important also to point out that whilst ontological, an experience of the self in the world also includes meaning-making which leads to ethical action. Kirmani and Kirmani (2009) note that participants indicated their concern regarding the destruction of natural environments due to industrial development, resulting in their resolve to 'go green' to protect the earth. Adams et al. (2008) also note how connectedness with nature encourages children to develop a sense of responsibility, thus inspiring them to consider their consumer choices and use of the existing world's resources. Known as biophilia, which is deemed to be an innate human capacity, and as significant as a child's relationships with people (Wilson, 1984), exposure to the wonder of the natural world evokes a sense of love for nature. This in turn inspires a response that leads to acts of sustainability and responsibility.

Finally, the *Cosmo-centric* spiritual sensitivity (Kirmani & Kirmani, 2009) picks up on the sense of mystery and awe, already suggested above, that is a hallmark of many discussions on children's spirituality and is a feature of educational policy in those contexts that do acknowledge spirituality as significant for the development of young children's lives. Hart suggests that these become the fabric of spiritual education noting how children have an inherent openness to mystery, wonder and delight. Whilst everyday experiences become the inspiration for this, spirituality grows when 'the individual consciousness opens up to the wider consciousness of which we are all a part' (Hart, 2003, p. 10). Hay and Nye additionally explore mystery-sensing as the inspiration for spiritual experience as outlined above. Within Kirmani and Kirmani's research (2009), participants identified instances where experiences beyond the self or immediate world had had an impact on their emotions and beliefs. Rays from the sun, a full moon, a sunset, thunder and the stars in the sky were all highlighted as the inspiration for feelings of wholeness, being moved and awe and wonder; but it is interesting to note that similar to the response to the *eco-centric* sensitivity, these experiences not only were meaningful in themselves, but were the catalyst again for meaningful action.

The authors (Kirmani & Kirmani, 2009, p. 376) write that some participants expressed concerns 'about the destruction of earth's atmosphere due to pollution, climate change and global warming' and describe how they 'reflected on their own responsibility in bringing about positive change to save the universe.' In relation to this, they suggest that practitioners might encourage children to use their reason and imaginations to ask questions about the cosmos, whilst also exposing them to experiences of wonder and awe. In response, children might explore the big questions of the universe through play and creativity, and going further, become acquainted with the various ways in which the natural environment might be maintained through sustainable practices and ecological behaviours.

In the light of the framework provided by Kirmani and Kirmani (2009), it might then be argued that as much as spiritual development in Early Childhood might bypass a cognitive approach to learning as described here, its significance must not be minimised. It is imperative that the potentiality for ethical behaviour that arises from spiritual being and experience, when authentic, is acknowledged as the starting point for a range of ethical and responsible behaviours, and it is the conjecture of this discussion that within Early Childhood Education, children's outdoor learning experiences can be considered as affordances for this.

Farrugia and Gellel (2022) similarly refer to ethical behaviour as resulting from a pedagogy that aspires for the transformation of individual learners and learning communities. From the starting point of everyday experience, which in this case includes outdoor learning, children are afforded opportunities to develop into their own humanity, or being, in two ways. First, within an emergent curriculum that allows for autonomous development, children might become reflexive participants in learning, engaging in, as already suggested earlier, questioning, criticality and the search for meaning. They are also encouraged to develop their own sense of self when given the opportunity to express themselves in a variety of means, described by Malaguzzi (Edwards et al., 1993) as the hundred languages of children. Yet further to this, children are afforded agency. In this, children are directors of their own learning, within a child-centred yet teacher-framed approach. As 'protagonists able to … take responsibility for their learning journey' (Farrugia & Gellel, 2022, n.p.), children's responses to their experiences can lead the way in the co-construction of classroom activities and further learning.

However, as stated above, reflexivity and agency also extend to children wanting to make a difference in the wider world. This is evidenced through literature pertaining to Education for Sustainable Development, which will be explored in due course. As much as it is questioned whether young children can understand and therefore engage with issues of sustainability, Pramling Samuelsson's research (2011) offers insights into the critical contribution that children make in response to global environmental issues, and reflecting on for example the responses of a class of pre-school children to the Australian wildfires and the plight of koala bears in the bush, she argues that children's voices should be not only heard on such issues, but in the first place, allowed in early years classrooms.

The notion of children and adults as co-learners is also proposed by Farrugia and Gellel (2022) within a relational route of spiritual development: this is highlighted alongside 'being' as significant in developing young children's spirituality. Along this route, which of course is not autonomous but ontologically linked to 'being' as Being-in-the-world (Heidegger, 1962), learning can facilitate deep connections with others. Farrugia and Gellel (2022) identify that within Early Childhood pedagogy, 'the environment is planned to nurture relationships' (Farrugia & Gellel, 2022, n.p.) and that through, for example, the project work that is a hallmark of the Reggio Emilia approach, a 'spiritual identity is constructed and negotiated through the interactions between children' (Farrugia & Gellel, 2022, n.p.) and others, be they parents, teachers, peers or pets.

The impact of spiritual experience

To conclude this chapter on children's spirituality, it is important to locate the hallmarks as described in the vignettes within a theoretical framework, to identify the impact of spiritual experience on young children's personal lives and development, and to advocate for the inclusion of spirituality within Early Childhood rhetoric and policy. Individuality and connectedness, wonder, corporeal and sensory experience and care have been addressed above, but engagement with other themes is necessary at this point: presence, imagination and creativity.

Presence. Immanent experiences or those which attend to the present, reminiscent of what Hay and Nye (2006, pp. 66–68) describe as the 'here and now,' have value for their own sake and for the inner life of the individual. Experiences are such as those described in the second vignette and encapsulated in the notion of 'flow.' Proposed by Csikszentmihalyi (1990, p. 3), the state of flow is considered as the 'optimal experience' where one is in control of consciousness to determine the contents of one's life. He writes that as the individual takes control of consciousness, one also can take control of the quality of an experience which in turn leads to personal liberation and happiness. Flow is also noted as a state in which people are so involved in an activity that nothing else seems to matter. It involves being 'in the moment' – away from the pressures of real life and within a dimension which appears to transcend time and space. Csikszentmihalyi (1990) makes a distinction between pleasure and enjoyment. In a pleasurable experience, nothing is changed as a result. An enjoyable experience, on the other hand, is one of accomplishment.

Certainly for the child in the second vignette, nature afforded the opportunity to experience presence. The intricacy of the flower petals and leaves provided a focus for attention, and as they closely observed, there was a sense of separation from the rest of the class that brought a sense peace. Lau (2009) considers this as mindfulness, and whilst not concerned with Early Childhood Education in particular, in her own context of Hong Kong, she advocates for mindful activity, such as mindful walking and mindful eating to be included within the curriculum for the well-being of all learners. As Csikszentmihalyi (1990) suggests, such a phenomenological approach to experience is required for well-being and happiness. However, meaning and value are concerned not with adherence to a higher authority but with what is already occurring in real life. In this respect, it has value within the Early Childhood curriculum, and I argue is relevant to practice and therefore policy.

Imagination

Gill Goodliff's concept of spiritual meta-environments (2016), considers non-physical spaces as instrumental in meaningful learning and development. Her assertion is that spirituality is mediated within three meta-environments: the friendship space, the imaginative narrative and the solitary imaginative. These conceptual spaces provide a representation of what Scott (2001) suggests is required for children to become aware of what is within, between and beyond themselves and others. Again, particularly here in relation to the imaginative aspect, children's experiences in nature provide a stimulus for the creation of a spiritual meta-space. For Goodliff (2016) the imaginative narrative includes exploring possibility, fantasy, and embodied expression. This includes imaginative play, through which aspects of rights, culture, and identity might be explored, also contributing to meaning-making. Imaginative play, she argues, establishes the open-ended nature of play against the 'market-driven creativity' of contemporary schooling and she advocates for a more democratic approach to learning, through which the 'humanising' principles of spirituality might be made manifest (Goodliff, 2016, p. 76).

In a further illustration, children at my school used their imaginations in the outdoor space to devise wild art – a picture created from leaves, sticks and stones. With no intended outcome, they were able to choose the materials from those they could find in the space and construct them as either a pattern or picture. Further to this, other learning was in evidence. They were experiencing how to negotiate in a democratic way – who will collect the materials, who will plan the picture, who will take the photograph? They used skills of evaluation and all worked together for a successful collective project. There was also evidence of them being in the moment – fully absorbed in the activity, reminiscent of the notion of flow (Csikszentmihalyi, 1990). Harris (2016) reinforces the importance of this meta-space, suggesting that young children have an incredible capacity for imagination, through which they can create solutions, solve problems and face new challenges. The outdoor space affords numerous opportunities for this.

Creativity

Mitton (1995), writing in relation to the spirituality of Celtic peoples, notes how creativity was an essential aspect of their life and worship. He writes: 'As the Celtic peoples were converted to Christ it must have been a great delight to them to find a faith that was so filled with creative life, affirming their delight in music and art' (Mitton, 1995, p. 65). The Celts communicated their spirituality in a variety of creative ways. Music, storytelling and poetry were all excellent vehicles for teaching Christian 'truth' but rather than promoting the tenets of faith through dogma, their belief was nurtured in a way that would 'not only feed the mind but would enlighten the spirit and warm the heart' (65). Therefore, underlining the development of spirituality, not only within religious communities but others, be they educational or social, creativity has a role.

Indeed, in the English *Early Years Foundation Stage Statutory Framework* (DfE, 2023), the opportunity for children to engage in Expressive Arts is encouraged, allowing children to 'explore and play with a wide range of media and materials' (DfE, 2023, p. 11). The document suggests that such activities develop language and other means of self-expression. Reflecting this, Eaude

(2009) asserts that the chance to play provides the opportunity for enormous pleasure. The significance of happiness, in relation to well-being, cannot be overstated. Moreover, it is through creativity that the individual discovers the self. Eaude writes: 'creativity requires the opportunity to experiment, to change and at times to fail, without the consequences being too severe' (2009, p. 194). Finally, emphasising the underpinning philosophical position of this chapter, Cremin et al. (2006) posit that through creativity, children might develop possibility thinking. This relates to the open-ended nature of learning, which in the outdoor space affords experimentation and collaboration. Fostering curiosity, autonomy and originality, creativity expressed through play becomes the means by which anything is possible for the children, and the channel through which new understanding and meanings can be made.

Concluding comments

As a practitioner and researcher within the field of children's spirituality, it is my conjecture that the innate spiritual sense that children have can inspire them to experience an awareness of a dimension both within and beyond themselves and that through an understanding of Being-in-the-world (Heidegger, 1962), connectedness with self, other and the world might inspire a sense of well-being and in turn social responsibility on the part of young children. The outdoor space acts as an affordance for this. Therefore, the discussion continues to explore the value of nature for young children before turning to outline the role of both nature and spirituality in the theories of Early Childhood pioneers.

References

Adams, K., Hyde, B. & Woolley, R. (2008). *The spiritual dimension of childhood*. London: Jessica Kingsley.
Adams, K., Monahan, J. & Wills, R. (2015). Losing the whole child? A national survey of primary education training provision for spiritual, moral, social and cultural development. *European Journal of Teacher Education*, 38(2), 199–216. https://doi.org/10.1080/02619768.2015.1030388
Adams, K., Bull, L. & Maynes, M.L. (2016). Towards an understanding of the distinctive features of young children's spirituality. *European Early Childhood Education Research Journal*, 24(5), 760–774. https://doi.org/10.1080/1350293X.2014.996425
Australian Government Department of Education. (2022). *Belonging, being and becoming: The early years learning framework for Australia (V2.0)*. ACT: Australian Government Department of Education for the Ministerial Council. Available from: https://www.acecqa.gov.au/sites/default/files/2023-01/EYLF-2022-V2.0.pdf
Bone, J., Cullen, J. & Loveridge, J. (2007). Everyday spirituality: An aspect of the holistic curriculum in action. *Contemporary Issues in Early Childhood*, 8(4), 344–354. https://doi.org/10.2304/ciec.2007.8.4.344

Buber, M. (1970). *I and thou.* New York: Charles Scribner's Sons.
Champagne, E. (2001). Listening to…Listening for…: A theological reflection on spirituality in early childhood. In J. Erricker, C. Ota & C. Erricker (Eds.), *Spiritual education. Cultural, religious and social differences, new perspectives for the 21st century* (pp. 76–87). Brighton: Sussex Academic.
Coles, R. (1990). *The spiritual life of children.* Boston: Houghton Mifflin.
Cremin, T., Burnard, P. & Craft, A. (2006). Pedagogy and possibility thinking in the early years. *International Journal of Thinking Skills and Creativity,* 1(2), 108–119. https://doi.org/10.1016/j.tsc.2006.07.001
Csikszentmihalyi, M. (1990). *Flow: The psychology of optimal experience.* New York: Harper and Row.
Department of Education, Employment and Workplace Relations [DEEWR]. (2009). *Belonging, being and becoming: Early years learning framework.* Available from: http://deewr.gov.au/early-years-learning-framework
Department for Education. (2023). *Early Years Foundation Stage Statutory Framework.* Available from: https://assets.publishing.service.gov.uk/media/65aa5e42ed27ca0 01327b2c7/EYFS_statutory_framework_for_group_and_school_based_providers .pdf.
de Souza, M. (2010). Meaning and connectedness: Australian perspectives on education and spirituality – An introduction. In M. de Souza & J. Rimes (Eds.), *Meaning and connectedness: Australian perspectives on education and spirituality* (pp. 1–6). Australia: Australian College of Educators.
de Souza, M., Cartwright, P. & McGilp, E.J. (2004). The perceptions of young people who live in a regional city in Australia of their spiritual wellbeing: Implications for education. *Journal of Youth Studies,* 7(2), 155–172.
Eaude, T. (2009). Happiness, emotional well-being and mental health – What has children's spirituality to offer? *International Journal of Children's Spirituality,* 14(3), 185–196. https://doi.org/10.1080/13644360903086455
Edwards, C., Gandini, L. & Forman, G. (1993). *The hundred languages of children: The Reggio Emilia approach to early childhood.* Norwood, NJ: Ablex Publishing Corporation.
Farrugia, K. & Gellel, A.M. (2022). Making young children's spirituality visible through an emergent approach. International Conference on Children's Spirituality (online).
Gelven, M. (1970). *A commentary on Heidegger's being and time.* New York: Harper and Row.
Gergen, K. (2009). *Relational being: Beyond self and community.* Oxford: Oxford University Press.
Goodliff, G. (2016). Spirituality in early childhood education and care. In M. de Souza, J. Bone & J. Watson (Eds.), *Spirituality across disciplines: Research and practice* (pp. 67–80). Netherlands: Springer. https://doi.org/10.1007/978-3-319-31380-1
Hardy, A. (1979). *The spiritual nature of man.* Oxford: Clarendon Press.
Harris, K. (2016). Let's play at the park! Family pathways promoting spiritual resources to inspire nature, pretend play, storytelling, intergenerational play, and celebration. *International Journal of Children's Spirituality,* 21(2), 90–103. https://doi.org/10 .1080/1364436X.2016.1164669
Hart, T. (2003). *The secret spiritual world of children.* Makawao: Inner Ocean Publishing.

Hay, D. & Nye, R. (2006). *The spirit of the child.* London: Jessica Kingsley Publishers.
Heidegger, M. (1962). *Being and time.* Oxford: Blackwell Publishers.
Heidegger, M. (1978). Letter on humanism. In M. Heidegger, *Basic writings.* London: Routledge.
HMSO. (1988). *Education reform act.* London: HMSO.
Hyde, B. (2008). *Children and spirituality: Searching for meaning and connectedness.* London & Philadelphia: Jessica Kingsley Publishers.
Hyde, B. (2022). Action possibilities enhancing the spiritual well-being of young children: Applying affordance theory to the Godly Play room. *Religions,* 13(12), 1202. https://doi.org/10.3390/rel13121202
Keltner, D. (2023). *Awe: The transformative power of everyday wonder.* London: Allen Lane.
Kirmani, M.H. & Kirmani, S. (2009). Recognition of seven spiritual identities and its implications on children. *International Journal of Children's Spirituality,* 14(4), 369–383. https://doi.org/10.1080/13644360903293630
Lau, N.-S. (2009). Cultivation of mindfulness: Promoting holistic learning and wellbeing in education. In M. de Souza, L.J. Francis, J. O'Higgins-Norman & D.G. Scott (Eds.), *International handbook of education for spirituality, care and wellbeing,* (pp. 715–737). Dordrecht: Springer.
Louv, R. (2005). *The last child in the woods: Saving our children form nature deficit disorder.* Chapel Hill, NY: Algonquin Books.
Mata-McMahon, J. & Escarfuller, P. (2023). *Children's spirituality in early childhood education.* New York: Routledge. https://doi.org/10.4324/9781003081463
McCreery, E. (1996). Talking to young people about things spiritual. In R. Best (Ed.), *Education, spirituality and the whole child* (pp. 196–205). London: Cassell.
Miller, J. (2000). *Education and the soul: Toward a spiritual curriculum.* Albany: State University of New York Press.
Miller, L. (2015). *The spiritual child. The new science on parenting for health and lifelong thriving.* New York: St. Martin's Press.
Mitton, M. (1995). *Restoring the woven cord.* London: Darton, Longman and Todd Ltd.
Otto, R. (1950). *The idea of the holy.* London: Oxford University Press.
Pramling Samuelsson, I. (2011). Why we should begin early with ESD: The role of early childhood education. *International Journal of Early Childhood,* 43, 103–118. https://doi.org/10.1007/s13158-011-0034-x
Robinson, C. (2019). Young children's spirituality: A focus on engaging with nature. *Australasian Journal of Early Childhood,* 44(4), 339–350. https://doi.org/10.1177/1836939119870907
Robinson, C. (2020). To be 'formed' and 'informed': Early years' educators' perspectives of spirituality and its affordance in faith-based early learning centres. *International Journal of Children's Spirituality,* 25(3–4), 254–271. https://doi.org/10.1080/1364436X.2020.1848810
Schein, D. (2018). *Inspiring wonder, awe and empathy: Spiritual development in young children.* St. Paul, MN: Redleaf Press.
School Curriculum and Assessment Authority [SCAA]. (1995). *Spiritual and moral development – SCAA discussion papers: No 3.* London: School Curriculum and Assessment Authority.
Scott, D. (2001). Storytelling, voice and qualitative research: Spirituality as a site of ambiguity and difficulty. In J. Erricker, C. Ota & C. Erricker (Eds.), *Spiritual*

education. *Cultural, religious and social differences, new perspectives for the 21st century* (pp. 118–129). Brighton: Sussex Academic.
Tacey, D. (2004). *The spirituality revolution: The emergence of contemporary spirituality*. Hove East Sussex: Brunner-Routledge.
Tubbs, N. (2005). *The philosophy of the teacher*. Oxford: Blackwell Publishing.
Wills, R. (2012). Beyond relation: A critical exploration of 'relational consciousness' for spiritual education. *International Journal of Children's Spirituality*, 17(1), 51–60. https://doi.org/10.1080/1364436X.2012.660747
Wilson, E.O. (1984). *Biophilia*. Cambridge, Massachusetts & London: Harvard University Press.

3 Children's spirituality, nature and Early Childhood foundations

Introduction

Learning outdoors currently forms a part of the development of pedagogies for young children across the globe. From the early pioneers to more recent research (e.g. Grenier & Vollans, 2023), the value of the outdoor space has been and continues to be an integral part of Early Childhood Education. Not only is nature considered essential for well-being and personal development, it also inspires a sense of social responsibility in young children and therefore is an essential part of early years teaching. This chapter explores the value of nature for young children's learning and development and considers the foundational philosophies of Early Childhood Education, as well as the role of outdoor learning within pedagogy and practice today.

The value of nature for young children

According to Greenman (2005), nature is universal and timeless. It is unpredictable, bountiful and alive with sounds; it nourishes and heals. Nature relates to a variety of spaces; therefore, it might be represented by a rainbow, a puddle, the coastline, a park, potted plants or herbs growing in a small area of a backyard or flowers on a window ledge. Engaging with nature can mean exposure to dramatic scenery including mountains and waterfalls, expansive landscapes or simply observing bugs on a log. It can involve experiencing sun, rain, storms, snow and ice, or noticing tiny drops of rain on a leaf; it might include following the flight of a bee or butterfly around a rose plant or a wildflower garden. According to Moss (2012), the range of natural spaces available outdoors are engaging, stimulating and life-enhancing environments where children can reach a new depth of understanding about themselves and their relationship with the world. In whatever way nature is experienced, it can encourage young children to see the world as 'fresh and new and beautiful, full of wonder and excitement' (Carson, 1962, p. 42).

This of course connects with material already explored concerning children's spirituality, which in the current discussion concerns an innate human state, noted in relation to Heidegger's philosophy as the basic state of

Being-in-the-world (Heidegger, 1962). Similarly, and again as already highlighted, the connection that children have with nature is also understood to be innate. This is recognised within the concept biophilia (Wilson, 1984). The hypothesis for this concept suggests that human beings have an intrinsic need for engagement with nature and as such, children have a primal impulse to connect to the natural world. Wilson equates biophilia to a force similar to gravity and implies that children are immediately drawn to natural features such as those listed in the paragraph above.

Moving away from an anthropocentric to a biocentric perspective, Wilson (1984) considers that all life on earth is interconnected, and rather than assuming the dominance of humans in ecological systems, each form of life is reliant on others for survival. He argues that any minimisation of exposure to nature can limit children's development, well-being and personal growth, and therefore, experiences of outdoor spaces are fundamental to childhood. Furthermore, Wilson asserts that experiences of nature lead to a love of nature. This is the starting point for children's critical thinking concerning environmental issues, and resonant of the description of care for animals inspiring a care for the world as illustrated in Chapter Two, it is suggested here that a love of nature can inspire critical thinking leading to responsible behaviour.

Due to the ever-changing environment, young children in the natural space can often express themselves freely. For example, as suggested in the previous chapter, they can communicate stories and feelings through dramatic play or natural art. Other benefits include being exposed to sunlight and open air, which positively impacts their immune system, bone development and physical activity levels (Bento & Dias, 2017). According to Bilton (2010, p. 40), outdoor learning can encourage 'young children to take risks, to overcome adversity, to think and make decisions confidently and to develop a strong sense of self-worth, self-regulation and self-motivation.' Bilton (2010), in line with Schein (2018), also suggests that the natural space can inspire awe and wonder, empathy, a creative attitude and a relationship with living things, all of which might encourage children to look outward, beyond themselves, to consider their interdependence with others.

However, certainly since the turn of the current century, there has been an increasing concern voiced by education and health-care professionals, and emphasised through the media, over the reduction of children's opportunities to access nature. A major factor has been the Covid-19 pandemic, which according to Pokhrel and Chhetri (2021) has caused a lot of strain on children's education and development due to school closures, compulsory isolating and social distancing when outside. Social and economic disparities across the world at the time of the global lockdowns from March 2020 onwards have meant that whilst access to outdoor space has been easily accessible for some, there are many others for whom experiencing nature has been a challenge. In Europe, children living in urban areas or in flats, for example, struggled to get outside throughout the pandemic (Lee et al., 2021). This suggests that although outdoor play has many additional benefits to children, it is not always accessible.

During the pandemic, the use of online resources became a key feature of daily life. This included the use of exercise videos and live sessions in promoting physical health (Winther & Byrne, 2020). Whilst this served a purpose at the time, there were potential problems with this in terms of young children's development. For example, when hiding, climbing and running, children expend energy and increase the heart rate, which in turn affords health benefits such as good sleep and a sense of well-being (Lambert et al., 2019). However, whilst short periods of exercise were allowed outside of the home, the reduction in the opportunity for physical activity particularly increased the risk of cardiovascular disease amongst young children as well as weight gain and depression (Lopez-Bueno et al., 2021). Children's physical health was further exacerbated by the transition to home-based online learning with many children engaging in their education using a laptop computer or tablet; therefore the limitation brought about by the pandemic often impacted on children's health in a less than positive way.

Both before the pandemic and since, barriers to children accessing nature have been identified. These include worries about safety and the rise in access to technology. Often safety concerns outweigh the need for risk and challenge in play, and while certain Early Childhood settings, for example, Forest Schools (a concept explored in Chapter Four), do indeed provide opportunities for risky play, an increase in traffic and concern about safeguarding often deter parents and carers from allowing their children to spend time outdoors. Gifford and Chen (2016), for example, propose that due to the proliferation of digital media and technology use especially on the part of young children, the amount of time they and their parents or carers are willing to spend outdoors is decreased; Radesky et al. (2015) additionally argue that smartphone or tablet use interferes with sensory-motor development and social interaction, each of which comes to the fore outdoors.

Louv, writing earlier in 2005, introduced the notion of nature-deficit disorder. In his book *Last Child in the Woods*, he cites current trends in education, with target setting prioritising academic success, as well as the evolving structure of towns and cities, as cultural and institutional barriers to children experiencing nature. He argues that personal and familial barriers such as commercialised and computerised play also contribute to this decline. Alongside the minimisation of risk, he identifies that the culture of litigation that is prevalent in Western European countries and beyond enforces a need to protect children's safety in educational and out-of-school activities and that an increasing sense of fear for children's safety limits their freedom and opportunity to engage with nature. Therefore, it is argued here that not only should learning in nature be prioritised in Early Childhood Education, but also encouraged in settings across all sectors and a range of international educational contexts.

Nature in the work of Early Childhood pioneers

It is important to note that many of the ideas concerning children's relationship to nature, and its subsequent value in both education and health care, are outlined in the work of pioneers within this field. Much Early Childhood literature concerning the relationship between nature and children's development, as well as nature and spirituality, has a basis in their philosophies. Therefore, the discussion at this point turns to a consideration of the work of Friedrich Froebel, Maria Montessori, Margaret McMillan and Susan Isaacs.

Friedrich Froebel (1782–1852), was a German educator historically known for the development of the 'kindergarten' (children's garden), and currently, his philosophy of education offers a welcome counterpoint to the neoliberal agenda that is increasingly influential in Early Childhood Education in this decade (see Chapter One). Rather than prioritising competition and testing within an outcomes approach, his child-centred principles encourage the education of the body, mind and spirit, with access to nature and the outdoors being a key component in the education of the whole child (Best, 2016). Indeed, according to Helenius (2023, p. 9), he 'was absolutely not satisfied with detached short-term narrow objectives.' Whilst Froebel's adult life involved him engaging in a range of occupations such as a teacher, personal tutor, architect and land surveyor, it was always his desire to understand and explore more deeply the complexities of life in relation to nature and the wider world that led him to develop a way of learning and understanding that became realised in the establishment of an educational community. Interestingly, he had little success in promoting his educational ideas within the school system; however, as his philosophy includes the view that the earliest years of a child's life lay the foundation for all later learning, and that later success depends on the development of personality, knowledge and skills in the early years, he turned his interest to this formative stage. This resulted in the establishment of the first kindergarten (Best, 2016). Akin to the idea of the growth of a bud into a flower or fruit given favourable conditions, within the kindergarten environment, children have the opportunity to fulfil their individual potential. The aim of education is thus personal as well as to support academic development (Helenius, 2023).

In the light of this, Froebel's approach includes an understanding of the inherent goodness of children, and as such education involves three forms of learning: knowledge of natural life, knowledge of forms (e.g. geometric shapes) and knowledge of beauty. Much of this takes place in the natural space. For example, the work of the kindergarten includes gardening and caring for animals, handiwork such as weaving and threading, singing and experimenting with colour and design (McDowall Clark, 2020). Additionally, a primary pedagogical tool is play. According to Campbell-Barr and Tregenza-May (2023), play involves children exploring, experimenting and being creative. Through play, they connect and communicate with others, develop

Children's spirituality, nature and Early Childhood foundations 45

positive relationships and build community. Through self-directed activity, they engage in problem-solving and discovery. Effective play is built on first-hand experiences of the world, through which young children can develop new understandings and meanings, leading to respect and responsibility for others and their environment. It also promotes positive mental health, and a sense of well-being and purpose.

As hallmarks of spirituality, these beneficial aspects of play reflect the experiences of the children described in the vignettes outlined in the Preamble. As such, it is possible to note how such aspects of children's spirituality might be afforded through play, and in this respect, Froebel's approach to learning might be considered as spiritual. As Best (2016) points out, Froebel's relationship with Christianity was evident within his work, yet his religion was not founded on the dogmatic principles of sin and salvation prevalent in German Lutheran churches at the time, but rather focused on the fulfilment on human life in relation to nature and the divine. This seems to reflect his pedagogical principles and it might be suggested that whilst personal growth is inspired through experiences in nature, so is religious awareness. Through the individual's engagement with the world, reflection affords entry to understanding 'the truth;' yet here, claiming truth is also considered ambiguous, not leading to accepting fixed determinates but embracing multi-layered meanings within cross-cultural experiences.

In exploring Froebel's spirituality, Tang and Zhao (2023) focus on the theme of unity embedded within his work, highlighting how spirituality involves connectedness of humanity, nature and divinity, through the relation of inner and outer worlds. Connectedness has the potential to inspire an ethics of care for self and others, as well as nature and the planet, and supports children to develop more diverse ways of thinking and understanding of the world. Acceptance and inclusion follow, within a world-view that considers all as equal, and all as responsible for others.

Alongside children engaging in personal growth and formation within a conceptual space, the purpose of Froebel's kindergarten is also that they take part in the growth of plant and animal life in the physical space. According to Best (2016), Froebel found that time working upon nature in the gardens was especially important. Additionally, Froebel found that through long and regular walks in the natural space surrounding the school, children would be able to find the true nature of all things as well as a deeper understanding of themselves and their place in the world. He felt that in nature a child's sensory experiences would help them to appreciate the grand design of the universe through experiencing opposites such as day and night and gaining a sense of the enormity of creation through observing the starry sky. Campbell-Barr and Tregenza-May (2023) suggest that growing flowers and food, and caring for animals induce a respect for the natural environment, leading to an awareness of climate and conservation issues. Therefore it is imperative that practitioners build on this within a pedagogy promoting sustainability. This theme will be developed further in Chapter Four.

In early 19th century Italy, Maria Montessori developed a pedagogy based on her conjecture that all children have an innate capacity for learning, nurtured when the environment, resources and methods are appropriate. She had a particular concern for children with disabilities and learning difficulties as well as children living in poverty, and in 1906 she was involved in the establishment of a school in an area of economic deprivation in Rome. This was named Casa dei Bambini (children's house). Montessori's pedagogy included the notion that within a carefully prepared environment, with adults scaffolding and modelling skills development, children would be able to play and work freely, leading their own learning whilst respecting boundaries and developing positive relationships. All activity is purposeful, and through attention and concentration, young children should not only gain knowledge and skills, but also regulate and develop a sense of control leading to agency (Feez, 2010).

Montessori's philosophy of education is often equated with the spiritual, and in the light of the discussion so far, connections can again be made between the vignettes of the Preamble and further development of ideas. First, in her book *Spontaneous Activity in Education*, the quote 'Our care of the child should be governed, not by the desire to make him learn things but by the endeavour always to keep burning within him that light which is called the intelligence' (2008, p. 240), resonates with the notion of an innate spirituality which inspires dynamic learning and development. Indeed, as Hay and Nye (2006) posit in relation to their model of 'relational consciousness,' it is from this foundational ontological state of being, that spiritual learning is then led forth.

Reflecting a contemporary concern, Montessori (2008) advocates for the promotion of the rights of young children – to be healthy, with their social needs met, protected but also given the opportunity for participation in self-development and awareness. She also advocates that the intellectual and physical development of children is not enough. She writes: 'With man the life of the body depends on the life of the spirit' (2008, p. 25), explaining that emotions such as grief, weariness, pleasure and anger contribute to both the physical and mental health of all humans including children, and that as such, attention should be given to nurturing the spiritual needs of learners.

Thus, potentiality and freedom are significant in Montessori's pedagogy. Again like the ideas explored in the previous chapter, such a spiritual education allows for not only personal development but transformation. She states: 'Free the child's potential and you will transform (him) into the world' (River House Montessori 2024, n.p.). Within the enabling environment and an active approach to learning, children can be empowered to explore their interests, foster their natural abilities and develop a strong sense of self. Rather than being moulded into fixed identities within a standardised approach within a performative paradigm, their potentiality through self-development, reflection, emotional development and a growing sense of responsibility can lead to empathetic relationships and a sense of responsibility. In turn, children can contribute to society, empowered to make a difference. Furthermore, in this approach, they are encouraged to ask existential questions in developing their sense of self, understanding that the world is complex and that there are many dimensions that might be critiqued. Montessori challenged the perspective of adult versus child, which in her time considered the child outside of society, and therefore not a citizen. She espoused the notion, counter-cultural at the time, that young children are key citizens whose role is to challenge and critique unsustainable normative ideas and practices (Boyd, 2018).

Nature and the outdoors are essential components of the Montessori pedagogy. According to Campbell-Barr and Tregenza-May (2023), the open-air space was beneficial to both the health and education of the children in her 'casa' whilst also drawing on their innate capacity to connect with the natural world. The authors continue to note that through work utilising natural materials and spaces, children can exercise freedom through imaginary and risky play, and that within an open-ended framework, they can experiment and work out solutions and strategies, thus developing a sense of responsibility. Montessori writes: 'There must be provision for the child to have contact with nature; to understand and appreciate the order, the harmony and the beauty in nature' (AIM 2024, n.p.) In *Spontaneous Activity in Education* (2008), she also suggests that a child's inner life unfolds in relation to external stimuli, for example observing nature, and that in response, utilising their freedom, they experience an 'awakening' leading to the development of positive behaviours or habit. These behaviours extend to care for the natural environment within which children, similar to the Froebelian approach, are encouraged to plant and grow flowers and food, care for animals and engage in activities to support sustainability.

For pioneers based in the UK, Margaret and Rachel McMillan, and Susan Isaacs respectively, considered nature and spirituality also to be essential to the development of their own Early Childhood settings. The McMillan sisters, living and working in Southeast London, within a similar historical and socio-economic context to Montessori, understood the benefits of outdoor education, fresh air and healthy eating on not only local children, but also their wider families. As advocates for free school meals, they were early thinkers regarding the connection of nutrition to academic attainment and personal growth, but more so understood how intergenerational education in healthy eating and cooking could reduce poverty and inspire further opportunities for children and their parents or carers (McDowall Clark, 2020). In England, the legacy of Margaret McMillan continues, with all school children up to the end of Key Stage One (age seven) having the opportunity for a free school meal, and current campaigns continuing to lobby for this to extend to all children in the Primary age group (up to age 11).

With the McMillan's original nursery opening in 1914 as the Open Air Nursery School, children were provided with opportunities for free play and exploration in a natural space, as well as camping and residential outdoor activities.

Not only was the outdoor space considered beneficial for health and well-being, as well as children's academic work, according to McDowall Clark (2020), it emphasised their sense of wonder. Again, as a hallmark of spirituality, wondering can lead to questioning, which then might promote a wider understanding of the world on the part of young children. Additionally, for Margaret McMillan (1930, cited in Grenier & Vollans, 2023), experiencing nature promoted the corporeal aspect of spirituality, emphasising that movement, including running, can inspire joy, thus enhancing young children's physical and mental well-being, but even more so, opening up their potential.

Susan Isaacs, working slightly later in the twentieth century, established the Malting House nursery in Cambridgeshire in 1924. Her pedagogy similarly aimed to stimulate the active enquiry of the children themselves rather than to teach them through a didactic approach, with her aim to bring learning within their immediate experience and to draw on their interests (Isaacs, 1930). She was an advocate for play, music and drama, and again considered the role of the environment as essential for supporting children's freedom. For Isaacs, later reflected by Malaguzzi in his Reggio Emilia approach to education, the environment is a teacher, and that under the guidance of adults who support, children can exercise freedom within a stimulating physical and conceptual space. For example, the garden in her nursery homed a playhouse, sandpit, chickens, rabbits and hens, as well as one of the first climbing frames in the country (McDowall Clark, 2020). For Isaacs, the outdoor space afforded children the opportunity to express themselves, including their feelings, thus supporting positive mental health. It also provided opportunities for social development and connectedness, valuing co-operation and collaboration, whilst also developing a positive relationship with nature. This included care for animals 'which teaches young children responsibility' (Giardiello, 2014, p. 107), with each child having their own vegetable plot to attend to. The use of imagination and emotional development were embedded within Isaac's pedagogy, and therefore whilst not explicitly suggesting so, the spiritual is again evident as an aspect of the children's experiences.

Early Childhood practice

In England, the outdoor space is considered to be central to young children's learning and development. The requirement to provide outdoor learning for all children is a feature of the *Early Years Foundation Stage Statutory Framework* (DfE, 2023, p. 36), with the obligation to:

> provide access to an outdoor play area. If that is not possible, they (providers) must ensure that outdoor activities are planned and taken on a daily basis (unless circumstances make this inappropriate, for example unsafe weather conditions).

Further to this, 'Understanding the World' as one of the seven areas of learning within this document, posits that 'guiding children to make sense of their physical world and their community' (DfE, 2023, p. 11), through outdoor learning such as visits to parks and other key aspects of society, will foster an understanding of the social, cultural, technological and ecological diversity within the world. Engaging with the natural world is a key part of this area, with the goals for achievement including young children being able to observe, draw and contrast aspects of nature, as well as understand natural processes and changes for example in the climate, seasons or matter.

It might be argued in light of the preceding discussion, however, that this offers a transactional, one-dimensional approach to children's engagement with nature, illustrating the performative agenda that seems to be increasingly seeping into Early Childhood Education. Any allusion to the sense of physical and mental well-being that nature affords is missing here and considering that the lockdown periods in 2020 and 2021 not only are a recent memory but formative times in the lives of our children just entering their school years, there is much here to critique. Grenier and Vollans (2023) warn against the dangers of being too activity-focused. They suggest that teachers are in danger of planning lessons that are too restrictive to creativity or experimentation to meet learning goals; however, they advise that practitioners maximise on young children's 'disposition to explore and learn about their world' and that activities should include open-ended tasks that build on their natural curiosity.

Nevertheless, within *Birth to 5 Matters*, the non-statutory guidance for the Early Years Foundation Stage (Early Education, 2021), a more balanced approach is outlined. This document focuses on the importance of the outdoor space in its promotion of well-being and inclusion, physical development, relationship building, a chance to relax, and the opportunity to make sense of the world, each of which again might be considered as spiritual. Additionally, *Birth to 5 Matters* (2021) emphasises how engagement with nature can promote a sense of responsibility, leading to young children becoming 'confident caretakers and problem-solvers of the future' (Early Education, 2021, p. 35). This then brings a transformative element to learning, one of the hallmarks of spiritual pedagogy considered in the previous chapter. This will be explored again further in Chapter Five. Akin to the perspective from the Early Childhood literature and practice of New Zealand, through heightened awareness and engagement with nature, children can become more responsible for the environment, leading to transformed behaviours for a sustainable way of life (Bone, 2016).

Pedagogical principles for nature and spirituality

As already introduced in the previous chapter, Early Childhood educator Deborah Schein (2018) touches on spirituality in relation to the sense of wonder evoked by nature. As well as arousing feelings that touch our inner lives and bring a sense of joy, she suggests that wonder as a verb implies a sense of amazement which can lead to curiosity or a desire to understand something greater than the self. She also relates this to a sense of mystery as children contemplate the beauty of both the immediate natural world and that which is unknowable, or not understood. Like others, Schein addresses the role of biophilia in Early Childhood Education, and, drawing on Wilson (1984), purports that children's experiences in the outdoor space instil a love of the earth and a love for life. This leads to their involvement in caring for the natural world and the living things within it. To facilitate all of this she suggests simply that children 'go outside every day!' (Schein, 2018, p. 90). On the other hand, in their recommendations to teachers concerning a spiritual pedagogy in Early Childhood settings, Mata-McMahon and Escarfuller (2023) promote the experience of nature indoors as an inspiration for young children's spiritual development. They relate this to the calming effect of natural objects as affordances of children's reflections and suggest that when bringing leaves and twigs into the classroom, or when planting and growing, children are engaging in spiritual activity.

Jane Bone's experience involves a way of life which embraces an intimate connection with nature. For herself, she notes that 'walking in the garden is its own meditation,' and ponders 'if only I could achieve this purity of living all the time' (2016, p. 253). This intimate connection embraces the individual and nature as one, much like Buber's 'I-thou' relation (1970) which has no borders. To support her assertion, Bone (2016) cites creation theologian Thomas Berry who suggests that his early childhood experiences provided him with an emotional attachment and intimacy with nature (for example, sitting in a meadow and feeling an attunement with the universe), experiences he describes as 'magic moments' (Bone, 2016, p. 247). In turn, these experiences of the outdoor space inspired a profound level of devotion to nature in his everyday life, leading to a passion for environmental advocacy and activism as an adult. Bone continues to suggest that similarly, young children's experiences of nature might inspire a willingness to take responsibility for the natural environment. She contests that 'early memories of forging a relationship with nature influence some people so that the environment may then become what they care about throughout life' (248). As such, engagement with nature can affect a child on a personal level but can furthermore have a transformative impact on the sustainability of the planet.

The notion of a 'magic moment' is further reflected in the work of Christopher Walton (2015). Working in a woodland activity and retreat centre in England, Walton engages young children in spiritual tasks undertaken within the centre's extensive grounds. One task includes children sitting in silence and solitude in nature. He writes that the participants 'sit, look, listen, smell, feel, think, watch and, if they want to, write or draw in their diaries at the time or later' (Walton, 2015, p. 5). He names this activity 'magic spots.' Walton prioritises this activity in its potential to sharpen non-verbal skills such as watching and waiting, and reflecting on interconnectedness with self, others and the world; the results of these experiences have included children's increased self-awareness, an enhanced appreciation of the natural world (such as the blueness of the sky or the sound of birds) and a regulation of thoughts. One child said in response to her magic spot: 'when I was there, sitting in all that silence with all the space, all my thoughts came flowing out of my brain, like I couldn't stop them' (6).

Finally, Kathleen Harris (2016) advocates for the promotion of the relational dimension of spirituality in nature, with the park as a particular play space. Writing with both families and practitioners in mind, she highlights how activities such as finding, observing, questioning and wondering can facilitate communication between peers or across generations, as well as curiosity, leading to a co-constructed learning task, and how through playing a team game or working together through a treasure hunt or flying a kite, empathy and co-operation might be developed. This relationship extends towards not just peers and adults, but also to animals and the earth itself. She suggests that when the premise is that the 'natural world is not separate but a part of who we are in the world, the child will then have the possibility to grow and honour his or her connection to the earth and also humanity' (Harris, 2016, p. 93).

Concluding comments

Through this book, it has been noted and will continue to note that young children's spirituality as an *a priori* dimension of human life is significant for their well-being, learning and development. It has been outlined that although in policies for Early Childhood Education in a range of countries, spirituality is at most implicit, whilst in others it is more explicit, there is evidence to suggest that the hallmarks of spirituality highlighted here might be recognised, furthered and developed within the Early Childhood curriculum. Furthermore, based on children's heightened spiritual awareness, which is often inspired in nature, opportunities for exploration and critical thinking within an open-ended pedagogy might encourage children to strive to make a difference in the world, through care for others and the environment. Three models for supporting such work are explored now, before my cycle of learning is introduced in the penultimate chapter.

References

AIM. (2024). Nature inspires learning. Available from: https://aimmontessoriteachertraining.org/solicitous-care-living-things/

Bento, G. & Dias, G. (2017). The importance of outdoor play for young children's healthy development. *Porto Biomedical Journal*, 2(5), 157–160. https://doi.org/10.1016/j.pbj.2017.03.003

Best, R. (2016). Exploring the spiritual in the pedagogy of Friedrich Froebel. *International Journal of Children's Spirituality*, 21(3–4), 272–282. https://doi.org/10.1080/1364436X.2016.1231664

Bilton, H. (2010). *Outdoor play in the early years. Management and innovation.* Abingdon: Routledge.

Bone, J. (2016). Environmental issues and spirituality: Tracing the past and making contemporary connections. In M. de Souza, J. Bone & J. Watson (Eds.), *Spirituality across disciplines: Research and practice* (pp. 245–258). Netherlands: Springer. https://doi.org/10.1007/978-3-319-31380-1

Boyd, D. (2018). Early childhood education for sustainability and the legacies of two pioneering giants. *Early Years*, 38(2), 227–239. https://doi.org/10.1080/09575146.2018.1442422

Buber, M. (1970). *I and thou.* New York: Charles Scribner's Sons.

Campbell-Barr, V. & Tregenza-May, S. (2023). Early years curriculum: Past, present and future trajectories. In C. Nutbrown (Ed.), *Early childhood education* (pp. 13–23). London: Sage.

Carson, R. (1962). *The silent spring.* Boston: Houghton Mifflin Company.

Department for Education. (2023). *Statutory framework for the early years foundation stage.* Available from: https://assets.publishing.service.gov.uk/media/65aa5e42ed27ca001327b2c7/EYFS_statutory_framework_for_group_and_school_based_providers.pdf

Early Education. (2021). *Birth to 5 matters: Non-statutory guidance for the early years foundation stage.* Available from: https://birthto5matters.org.uk/wpcontent/uploads/2021/04/Birthto5Matters-download.pdf

Feez, S. (2010). *Montessori and early childhood: A guide for students.* London: Sage.

Giardiello, P. (2014). *Pioneers in early childhood education: The roots and legacies of Rachel and Margaret McMillan, Maria Montessori and Susan Isaacs.* London: Routledge.

Gifford, R. & Chen, A. (2016). Children and nature – What we know and what we do not. Available from: https://lawson.ca/wp-content/uploads/2018/04/Children-and-Nature-What-We-Know-and-What-We-Do-Not.pdf

Greenman, J. (2005). *Caring spaces, learning spaces.* 2nd ed. Redmond, WA: Exchange Press inc.

Grenier, J. & Vollans, C. (2023). *Putting the EYFS curriculum into practice.* London: Sage.

Harris, K. (2016). Let's play at the park! Family pathways promoting spiritual resources to inspire nature, pretend play, storytelling, intergenerational play, and celebration. *International Journal of Children's Spirituality*, 21(2), 90–103. https://doi.org/10.1080/1364436X.2016.1164669

Hay, D. & Nye, R. (2006). *The spirit of the child.* London: Jessica Kingsley Publishers.

Heidegger, M. (1962). *Being and time.* Oxford: Blackwell Publishers.

Helenius, A. (2023). Froebel for me. In T. Bruce, Y. Nishida, S. Powell, H. Wasmuth & J. Winnett (Eds.), *The Bloomsbury handbook to Friedrich Froebel* (pp. 7–9). London: Bloomsbury Publishing.

Isaacs, S. (1930). *Intellectual growth in young children.* London: Routledge.

Lambert, A., Vlaar, J., Herrington, S. & Brussoni, M. (2019). What is the relationship between the neighbourhood built environment and time spent in outdoor play? A systematic review. *International Journal of Environmental Research and Public Health*, 16(20), 3840. https://doi.org/10.3390/ijerph16203840

Lee, E., Bains, A., Hunter, S., Ament, A., Brazo-Sayavera, J., Carson, V., Hakimi, S., Huang, W., Janssen, I., Lee, M., Lim, H., Silva, D. & Tremblay, M. (2021). Systematic review of the correlates of outdoor play and time among children aged 3-12 years. *International Journal of Behavioural Nutrition and Physical Activity*, 18, 41. https://doi.org/10.1186/s12966-021-01097-9

López-Bueno, R., López-Sánchez, G.F., Casajús, J.A., Calatayud, J., Tully, M.A. & Smith, L. (2021). Potential health-related behaviours for pre-school and school-aged children during COVID-19 lockdown: A narrative review. *Preventive Medicine*, 143, 106439. https://doi.org/10.1016/j.ypmed.2020.106349

Louv, R. (2005). *The last child in the woods: Saving our children form nature deficit disorder*. Chapel Hill, NY: Algonquin books.

Mata-McMahon, J. & Escarfuller, P. (2023). *Children's spirituality in early childhood education*. New York: Routledge. https://doi.org/10.4324/9781003081463

McDowall Clark, R. (2020). *Childhood in society for the early years*. 4th ed. London: Sage.

Montessori, M. (2008). *Spontaneous activity in education*. Available from: https://www.gutenberg.org/cache/epub/24727/pg24727-images.html

Moss, S.M. (2012). Natural childhood. Available from: http://www.nationaltrust.org.uk/document-1355766991839

Pokhrel, S. & Chhetri, R. (2021). A literature review on impact of COVID-19 pandemic on teaching and learning. *Higher Education for the Future*, 8(1), 133–141. https://doi.org/10.1177/2347631120983481

Radesky, J., Schumacher, J. & Zuckermann, B. (2015) Mobile and Interactive media use by young children: The good, the bad and the unknown. *Paediatrics*, 135(1), 1–3. https://doi.org/10.1542/peds.2014-2251

River House Montessori. (2024). Famous Maria Montessori quotes. Available from: https://riverhousemontessori.edu.vn/famous-maria-montessori-quotes/

Schein, D. (2018). *Inspiring wonder, awe and empathy: Spiritual development in young children*. St. Paul MN: Redleaf Press.

Tang, F. & Zhao, J. (2023). Spirituality in early childhood pedagogy: A Froebelian Lens on the role of women in a Chinese context. In T. Bruce, Y. Nishida, S. Powell, H. Wasmuth & J. Winnett (Eds.), *The Bloomsbury handbook to Friedrich Froebel* (pp. 372–380). London: Bloomsbury Publishing.

Walton, C. (2015). Childhood awaits every person. *International Journal of Children's Spirituality*, 20(1), 4–14. https://doi.org/10.1080/1364436X.2014.999228

Wilson, E.O. (1984). *Biophilia*. Cambridge, Massachusetts & London: Harvard University Press.

Winther, D. & Byrne, J. (2020). Rethinking screen-time in the time of Covid-19. Available from: https://www.unicef.org/innocenti/stories/rethinking-screen-time-time-covid-19

4 Children's spirituality, nature and Early Childhood practice

Introduction

Having considered the value of nature for young children's learning and development, which includes the promotion of spiritual awareness in relation to identity, connectedness and care for others and the world, this chapter connects to research and practice within contemporary Early Childhood Education. Three examples will be explored: Education for Sustainable Development, Forest Schools and Eco Schools. Each offers an example of how researchers and practitioners might evidence the value of outdoor learning in relation to social responsibility and well-being. There additionally is a degree of criticality in this chapter, since such pedagogical models might be contested in the light of the understanding of children's relationship to nature within, for example, Indigenous communities. Furthermore, with the models as fixed entities in themselves, it is considered in due course how the methods mooted here might be at odds with the notions of freedom and agency promoted by the Early Childhood pioneers of the previous chapter. Nevertheless it is important to highlight current practice, and this begins with an exploration of Education for Sustainable Development (ESD).

Education for Sustainable Development

A recent development in Early Childhood Education in relation to both nature and social responsibility is Education for Sustainable Development (ESD). Indeed, according to Nikiforidou et al. (2020), early years educators have an essential role in encouraging a response to issues concerning the environment, so as to promote the values of responsibility for a sustainable world.

ESD has its foundations in the report from the Brundtland World Commission on Environment and Development: *Our Common Future* in which sustainable development is identified as that which 'meets the needs of the present without compromising the ability of generations in the future to meet their own needs' (WECD, 1987, p. 43). This means that within their own temporality and experience of the now, learners might engage in activities or behaviours that impact the world in the future, hopefully in positive ways.

According to Kemp (2018), the report emphasises the needs of the world's poor and highlights how social structures and technologies must be re-evaluated to meet these needs in the present and future.

ESD also has resonance with the 17 Sustainable Development Goals launched by the United Nations (United Nations, 2015), designed as a model to be used in creating an equitable approach across member countries to promote a sustainable environment for the future. These goals include eradicating hunger, as well as ensuring clean water and sanitation, reduced inequalities and responsible production and consumption. Additionally, the United Nations Convention on the Rights of the Child (United Nations, 1989) states that all children have the right to good quality health care, clean water, nutritious food and a clean healthy environment. They should also be free from neglect, harm and abuse, with the right to an education, the right to play, and the right to freedom of expression.

Children's rights resonate with the Sustainable Development Goals. Both Pramling Samuelsson (2011), and Yarwood and Tyrell (2012) indicate how issues relating to climate change and the environment impact these rights for children around the world. As such, they argue that through education, children should be empowered to have input within their own environments and in relation to their own cultural contexts. It is imperative that their voices are heard and their perspectives appreciated, as it is the voices of those whose futures are affected that should be included in the creation of opportunities for further development.

Additionally, in 2021, the significance of education was highlighted at a world conference on Sustainable Development, at which it was proposed that even the youngest children, when introduced to issues concerning the endangered planet, can respond and in turn become agents of change (Grenier & Vollans, 2023). This resonates again with the principle of Pramling Samuelsson (2011), who believes that children should be viewed as competent and communicative individuals with cognitive abilities and resources fully able to contribute to the present and future of the planet. Similarly, Nikiforidou et al. (2020) suggest that ESD involves children learning and addressing concerns *about* the environment, followed by action *for* the environment, engendering respect for the world and others, in the present and for future generations. Therefore, educators must build on children's individual everyday experiences to be able to participate in their education and have input to discussions and decisions about what is important to them.

Sustainability is not an easy concept for children to understand, and research indicates that amongst practitioners there is a lack of knowledge leading to its omission within planning and teaching. Furthermore, as it is not a discrete subject, but implicit within all curriculum areas, there is a danger that the principles become absorbed within the whole learning experience, without particular attention to its values (Grenier & Vollans, 2023). In this respect, it is helpful to consider ESD as the inter-relationship of three pillars, each of which contributes to sustainable development. The environmental pillar involves education about the natural environment, including the protection of ecosystems, biological diversities and pollution. The socio-cultural pillar involves equality, diversity, human health, education, poverty and justice. The economic pillar includes aspects such as poverty, disability, well-being, gender inequalities and human rights (Kemp, 2018). The issues included within each pillar do stand alone, but the strength of ESD is in the relationship between them which promotes values, practices and behaviours for a sense of justice, responsibility and dialogue.

However, sustainability, as spirituality, is not easily understood or explained. It is also subjectively and contextually interpreted, therefore it is difficult to write about it in universal terms (Kemp, 2018). Of course, climate change and the implications of rising temperatures across the world affect many. Yet the views of developed countries on the need for sustainable activity will differ greatly from those whose daily lives are framed by the experiences or aftermath of extreme weather and natural disasters. Hence, it is important to note that when considering ESD in Early Childhood Education, it is unhelpful to make generalisations and assumptions concerning geographical or cultural situations, and equally unhelpful to adopt an approach that considers children in the developing world as recipients of goodwill in a way that takes away their own agency and ability to educate and be educated for social change. Therefore, globally, all children can function as responsible citizens in working towards the Sustainability Goals.

Again, the belief that even the very young can critically evaluate social behaviours to make a change is integral to ESD (Pramling Samuelsson, 2011). According to Featherbe et al. (2023), the challenge for practitioners in Early Childhood Education is to develop pedagogical practices that support the promotion of the issues within the three pillars without being overly directive. As we know from the theory of play, children develop ideas based on their existing understandings of the world. As Else (2009) states, 'children choose the content and purpose of their actions, following their own instincts, ideas and interests, in their own way for their own reasons' (Else, 2009, p. 11). Therefore, resonating with the view of Sen (1996, cited in Featherbe, Lloyd-Evans and Moylett, 2023), an intentionality is required in terms of highlighting the issues whilst at the same time promoting a 'capability-centred' approach through which the children can integrate sustainable ideas within their own freely directed play. Nikiforidou et al. (2020), endorse this idea, positing that ESD should be supported through a play-based curriculum alongside the promotion of knowledge and understanding. They suggest for example that role play, picture books, art and music might provide responsive activities and that such activities should 'provide opportunities for communication, participation and interaction' (Nikiforidou et al., 2020, pp. 114–115).

Underpinning this, from a spiritual and philosophical perspective, is the notion of Being (Heidegger, 1962). As Kemp (2018) explains, it is when children are considered as constantly existing in the state of being in relation to becoming, that they might be identified as agents for change. Reflecting the definition of sustainable development as stated in the Brundtland Report (WCED, 1987), children's 'being' allows them to critically reflect on the issues they learn about or experience first-hand, and as beings who also exist in a state of becoming, they have the ability to act on their reflections in their play (or writing, creativity, experimenting, drawing and other suitable activities), leading to the creation of new understandings and therefore social behaviours (Kemp, 2018). These are not limited to environmental issues, but equally include socio-cultural attitudes and economic activities which benefit not just themselves in their own temporality but the lives of others beyond the immediate.

In relation to the philosophy of Heidegger (1962) introduced in Chapter Two, and to be explored further in the next chapter, this reflects the idea of a child's existence including their potentiality-for-Being (*Dasein*) within the ontological state of Being-in-the-world. As ESD takes place within the children's own communities and localities, it is meaningful therefore not just to themselves as individuals but also to their primary carers and others in their immediate environment (Nikiforidou et al., 2020), and in some cases the wider world.

It is important that examples from practice are provided to illustrate how ESD might be recognised and given more traction in Early Childhood Education, but also how, within an understanding of the ontological state of Being (Heidegger, 1962), children's spirituality might also provide the starting point for this mode of teaching and learning.

Within the writing of Pramling Samuelson (2011), an example is provided by Ruth Wallbridge, an early years teacher in Australia, who wondered if at such an early age, children were able to 'think beyond themselves' (2011, p. 105). Following her question about the children's wishes for the world, she was amazed to hear the responses. One child said: 'I wish people didn't cut down trees because that makes koalas and monkeys die,' whilst another stated: 'I wish that no one could throw rubbish on the earth because it makes the earth sick, and if it can't get better, we will die' (105). In terms of the development of a child's maturity, Pramling Samuelsson (2011) thus presents the opinion that a pre-school child *is* aware of such issues and thus has the ability to understand sustainability. The quotes also illustrate how young children understand the world and the impact that their actions can have on their environment. The author does note that of course, the understanding of a three-year-old will differ from that of an adult; however, she makes the point that children should not be sheltered from the difficulties in life and that 'windows of opportunity' should be provided for them to make sense of the issues of the world (Pramling Samuelsson, 2011, p. 106).

In my own village, children in the local pre-school told their teachers of their concerns about the mess made by dogs on the pavements. This is an issue that they have more than likely heard adults discuss, but it was also something that they wanted to see changed. As a response, the teachers led the children in an activity whereby plastic bottles were cut up, decorated and filled with doggy waste bags. The children and staff walked around the local area, and tied the bottles on lamp posts so that dog walkers could help themselves to a bag if needed to keep the environment clean. Again, in the light of the examples outlined above, the children collaborated with their teachers to identify problems and create a solution.

It is important as a final comment on ESD that as Nikiforidou et al. (2020) point out, teachers become committed themselves to learning about and embracing appropriate economic, political, social and environmental issues. Additionally, training must be developed to encourage early career teachers, especially to be able to listen to children when they raise their concerns, and to be able to respond in a way that supports learning within an established framework, yet also acknowledges their voices and desire to affect change. Promoting outdoor play in nature is one way to encourage children to think and act sustainably; through creativity, co-operative activities and experiences, children will indeed be able to become agents of social change.

Forest School

Forest School is a growing concern internationally for children of all ages, although its premise is closely aligned with Early Childhood pedagogy and practice. The concept has its roots in the free air life approach to Early Childhood Education seen in Denmark (European Scandinavia), in which children are given opportunities to play and explore freely in a natural outdoor space. The label 'Forest School' does not in fact exist in Denmark; in this context, outdoor learning is implicit within the practices and programmes of kindergartens and other pre-school settings. Rather, the concept has evolved as a popular aspect of outdoor learning in the UK and other countries, and whilst it is not a carbon copy of the Danish approach, it includes the range of values and practices, such as team-building and risk-taking, observed by teachers and researchers visiting Denmark in the early 1990s (Williams-Siegfredsen, 2017). The first iteration of a Forest School is noted as being established for early years children in Bridgewater School, Somerset in the UK in 1993; meanwhile, it is now possible for schools to become recognised Forest School providers (Forest School Association, 2024), although the underlying values are implicit within much early years teaching and learning across various contexts. For example, developing interest is evident across contexts such as Portugal, USA, Canada, Australia, Greece, China and Spain (Williams-Siegfredsen, 2017).

As noted by Garden and Downes (2023), the Forest School label represents an approach to education in natural environments with the intention that children's personal qualities are encouraged and developed within the outdoor space, and the perceived outcome that this would have a positive impact on mental health and well-being. Knight (2016) also notes how outdoor learning might be efficacious for some children, for example, those with special educational needs and disabilities or those with emotional and/or behavioural difficulties as well as children of pre-school age or the youngest children in a primary school. The pedagogical principles of Forest School resonate also with the ideas within this current discussion, with the Forest School Association website (Forest School Association, 2024, n.p.) indicating that the child-centred approach aims to allow learners to 'develop socially, emotionally, spiritually, physically and intellectually.' It also encourages a meaningful connection to the world, inspiring children to reflect on their place within it; as a result, learners develop self-esteem, resilience and problem-solving skills.

In a way that might be perceived as contradictory to the risk-averse culture certainly gaining traction in Early Childhood policy (see Chapter One), in the Forest School approach, children are encouraged to engage in risk-taking activities such as climbing trees or working with tools (Cooke et al., 2021). Furthermore, through collaboration and teamwork, children can develop new friendships as well as rehearse interpersonal skills such as sharing, negotiation and listening. The experiential dimension of this approach sets up a distinction from a curriculum-based outcomes approach, and as Knight (2016) suggests, practitioners might counter-balance performativity with the outdoor play and exploration that lack intended outcomes. Such activity might again be deemed as promoting spiritual awareness (see Preamble), allowing children to reflect on their relationships with others.

Garden and Downes (2023) also note the impact of well-being on children enhanced through this pedagogy. They draw on the research of Tiplady and Menter (2020, cited in Garden & Downes, 2023) that highlights the positive impact of Forest School on children experiencing emotional anxiety and those for whom attending mainstream school was a challenge. It might be fair to assume that as the open, therefore less imposing, environment has the potential for more person-centred learning, with outcomes driven by the individual rather than a fixed curriculum, the benefits for a number of children will become increasingly apparent. Finally, the authors, drawing on research undertaken by Turtle, Convery and Convery (2015, cited in Garden & Downes, 2023), note that children who have extensive long-term experience in Forest School tend to develop more environmentally responsible views leading to their involvement in sustainability. This again echoes earlier detail within this book, underlined by the understanding within the concept of biophilia (Wilson, 1984) that an experience of nature can lead to a love of and responsibility for the natural environment. As Knight (2016) points out, the Forest School approach sits comfortably alongside ESD and in conclusion, it might be highlighted that such learning also demonstrates the hallmarks of children's spirituality as already explored, including the impact of spiritual experience on young children's beliefs, values and behaviours.

A first example comes from Australia. Based on their research, Elliot and Chancellor (2014) reflect on the significance of a Bush Kinder programme implemented by staff from a kindergarten located in a suburb of Melbourne in the state of Victoria. Approximately two kilometres from the setting, a natural site affords the opportunity for a Forest School style approach to learning in a natural environment, with native bush, trees and rocks available for free play. During the research period, children took part in regular and lengthy sessions (three hours weekly) in the natural environment. The learning goals were aligned to the Early Years Learning Framework (DEEWR, 2009 cited in Elliot & Chancellor, 2014) yet exercised in the spirit of affordance theory (Gibson, 1986, cited in Elliot & Chancellor, 2014), in which a call-and-response style relationship was established between the formal aspects of provision and the children's interpretations of their experiences. Reflecting on the sessions, teachers noted how the environment had a calming and levelling effect on children and staff, that they developed more meaningful and inclusive attitudes towards others, as well as a deeper connectedness to the natural world, and more positive attitudes towards the environment. There are echoes here of ESD, and equally, children's spirituality. As one parent noted, it was noticeable how simplicity and peace pervaded the sessions, and that the children were enlightened, 'literally getting a feeling for nature' (Elliot & Chancellor, 2014, p. 50).

The final illustration is from my own experience of Forest School. My child, who has a learning disability, attended a school which is a recognised provider. Often, parents and carers were invited to join in with the children's teaching and learning sessions, and on one occasion, such a session took place in the Forest School area. The task was for the learners to collect wood (branches, sticks, leaves etc.) to make a fire. They could work in pairs, individually or in small groups. It was evident that some found this challenging from a social perspective. There was some hesitation where learners did not want to work in a group or pair but were also anxious to work alone, with other situations where working in a pair was causing conflict. There was little intervention, however, on the part of staff, as one aspect of the pedagogy here was to allow the learners to work out their own solutions to the problems. After almost half an hour, enough wood was collected and a small fire was built. The teacher lit the fire, and as soon as the wood began to burn, there was immediately a feeling of unity amongst the group. All looked in wonder at the flames spreading quickly through the sticks and leaves, and as they gasped 'wow' the difficulties of the previous thirty minutes were superseded by this intense moment of joy and amazement.

Eco-Schools

A third aspect of Early Childhood Education that provides evidence of the value of outdoor learning in relation to well-being and social responsibility is the 'Eco-Schools' initiative. Through this initiative, my own school has worked towards and achieved the Green Flag accreditation, complete with a green flag flying high at the front of the building, indicating that we have evidenced seven principles in practice. These include establishing an eco-committee, monitoring the use of resources and the impact of activities on the environment, making links to and from the established curriculum and involving the wider community (Eco-schools, 2024). According to Korkmaz and Yildiz (2017), Eco-Schools programmes are implemented in 56 countries, including their own context of Turkey. The goal of International Eco-Schools is to raise environmentally conscious individuals (Cincera et al., 2015), who have gained skills for thinking about environmental issues.

Again, as with the Forest Schools approach there is a clear resonance with both ESD and spirituality, and as Korkmaz and Yildiz (2017) point out, both research (for example Pramling Samuelsson, 2011) and policy (UNESCO, 2020) advocate for such environmental education to be integrated within Early Childhood learning opportunities. In terms of ESD, Korkmaz and Yildiz (2017) highlight how the Eco-Schools programme equips children with the values of compassion and empathy, which in turn influence their behaviours so they can consider sustainability and social justice in their daily lives. In relation to spirituality, Eco-Schools sessions provide a conceptual space in which children can reflect on their understanding of the world and critique the behaviours of humans in relation to the planet. They consider ways of acting for change through child-led activities, planned in response to learner's own reflections and passions.

Using my own school setting again as an example, through ideas inspired by the Eco-council, children engage in a range of activities to monitor the behaviour of both staff and students. For example, volunteers audit which classes still have the lights on when empty and monitor the amount of paper that goes into general waste rather than the recycling bin. Through the weekly newsletter, children write ideas for sustainability such as how to recycle crisp packets and offer ideas for crafts that re-use cardboard or plastic items found in the home. Every half term there is a book swap, and weekly, a child in each class takes it in turns to take home an eco-diary. This allows them to consider pertinent environmental issues and record their responses. These are then shared with the class back in school. The results of children's reflections and responses lead the way in inspiring class activity and to date, these have included tasks such as creating musical instruments from plastic bottles, planting seeds and creating a display wall full of recycled materials. A whole school recycling scheme has also emerged through the lessons.

A number of these activities are reflected in the research of Cincera et al. (2015), whose article was written from the context of the Czech Republic and explores the attitudes of kindergarten children towards environmental issues following the implementation of an Eco-Schools programme. Mostly the children's attitudes were positive, evidencing pro-environmental attitudes and behaviours. The researchers noted how children enjoyed connecting with nature through excursions and visits to local natural sites. Some worked in the school garden and others acted as 'inspectors' who monitored the use of resources, for example turning off taps. A recycling scheme was established and in collaboration with parents and teachers, children designed gardens for a sustainable future. In analysing feedback from teachers following the sessions, several questions were raised concerning the authenticity and effectiveness of this approach, especially in relation to the power dynamics between adults and children, and how the intended outcomes were reached. Nevertheless, the researchers also noticed that when an emancipatory approach was applied to the sessions, which encouraged children to 'set their own environmental agenda and suggest simple actions for improving the local environment or solving environmental problems' (Cincera et al., 2015, p. 922), 'children's pro-environmental attitudes increased' (931). This change in attitude might be considered as transformative, and whilst it is not possible to generalise based on this research, there are indications here of the impact that exposure to nature and activities supporting environmental concerns can have on children's views and in turn behaviours.

A final example from my own school concerns food waste. The younger children in school, especially close to the beginning of the year, find it hard to eat their lunches. In the UK, all children up to the end of their third year in school can have a free cooked dinner on site. However, as the children aged four and five are still developing the motor skills required such as cutting and holding a knife and fork correctly in order to eat their lunch, a lot of food is wasted. Older children however, having experienced Eco-Schools sessions throughout their time in the setting, wanted to ensure that the children were able to manage their food effectively enough to limit waste. Therefore, a few volunteers offered to spend some of their own play time sitting with the young children, offering support and befriending them to help them eat their whole meal. This pupil-led initiative reflects the sense of personal responsibility shown by the older children towards the youngest in the school.

As highlighted above, the spiritual quality of connectedness is evident here. As Cincera et al. (2015) note, through Eco-Schools, children can experience both a meaningful connectedness with the natural environment and other learners. In addition, the emancipatory aspect of this programme is deemed significant. In relation to the current discussion, it is important to note how an understanding of Being in relation to education is considered the starting point for meaningful learning. Being is also how connectedness, reflection and transformation occur. A philosophical exploration of this process is offered in the following chapter.

Criticality: cultural and social inclusion

It is important to note that a volume such as this, which is written from the context of the UK but with a potential global reach, is self-critical in terms of the Western lens through which nature, spirituality and Early Childhood are explored. As alluded to in an earlier chapter, listening to the voices of Indigenous learners and leaders is essential (Robinson, 2019) as well as ensuring that practice is reflective of the multi-layered cultures within which children live. For example, from an Australian context, Gillan et al. (2017) note a lack of progress in knowledge and skills across the curriculum on the part of Indigenous children, suggesting that the educational frameworks offered to children in this context are increasingly less relevant to their own identities and culture. The authors suggest that a way forward is for the social and historical context of these learners to be integrated with pedagogy, curriculum and assessment in schools; part of this strategy includes investment in Early Childhood Education which uses culturally appropriate resources and an intergenerational approach to ensure that learning starts with families, supported by schools, to encourage young children to become school ready.

One aspect of ESD already highlighted is the socio-cultural pillar. Through an awareness of this, inclusive practice, which concerns education with and for children from a range of cultural backgrounds, as well as those with disabilities and non-normative lived experiences, should be implicitly embedded within all Early Childhood Education. Again, attention to cultural diversity through singing, artwork, storytelling, drama and other creative methods brings the global into the local. Children's picture books and videos, visitors and field trips are all interesting ways of supporting cultural education. The outdoor space, as noted above, as an open-ended environment, is itself inclusive and whilst for some children, exploring and risk-taking are the preferred activities, for others, quiet reflection, focusing and noticing are meaningful.

However, it must be appreciated that the language of inclusion might also be contested. According to Bleeksma and Boumann (2024), an inclusive practice which perpetuates meanings based on those understood in the Global North inevitably operates differently to the experiences of the Global South, thus establishing a false expression of community. Indeed, as promoted through the work of Barbara Rogoff (2003), which is critical of the dominance of Global North thinking in terms of constructs of childhood and child development, learning experiences should not just *include* elements of the lived experiences of others but become expressions of them. Through her concept of 'pitching in,' (Rogoff & Megia-Arauz, 2022), Western individualisation is overcome by the participatory action taking place within communities and inter-generational relationships. Therefore, when reflected in the Early Childhood setting, the priority here is on young children, in collaboration with adults and members of the community, taking responsibility, participating in and contributing to society.

This is further reflected in the ethnographic research of Karen Ann Watson-Gegeo (Gegeo & Watson-Gegeo, 2001) concerning the Indigenous Kwara'ae people of the Solomon Islands in Oceana, and how their young relate to the natural environment in an authentic way. For example, she notes how children take part in agricultural activity from the age of three. This 'work' includes carrying heavy loads of wood, building fires, collecting water and cutting grass; to carry out these tasks they are skilled users of a child-sized machete. From the age of five, children can plant and grow their own food, which can be harvested to use in cooking or selling, and they can begin to raise and nurture animals. In these Early Childhood years, the children are playing while working, that is, being creative and imaginative, and using the skills of co-operation and independent thinking. Yet they are also expressing themselves in relation to their own context, therefore authentically.

From a research perspective, Gegeo (Gegeo & Watson-Gegeo, 2001), a Pacific Islander herself, suggests that local peoples must become involved in constructing local epistemologies. She suggests that local peoples must become involved in validating their own ways of knowing and being and identifies that through writing and recording about their identity and culture, they become the authors of their own data rather than being subject to outsider research. This is as important for education as it is for research, and further exploration of this idea is required to inform Early Childhood Education in a wider range of contexts globally.

In terms of the language of inclusion, it is important to note that albeit often inadvertently, this can establish a dualism between two groups of people – the normative and non-normative. This is problematic in that a deficit model becomes prevalent for those who are different from the majority but are encouraged to become accepted, or even acceptable, within the dominant paradigm. Attention to aspects of their own lived experiences does offer some concession towards what they can offer; however, it is rare that learning is established fully on their terms. 'Inclusion' then can become guilty of the tokenism that might reinforce some children as 'other' (Wills, 2021). As Dunne (2009) argues, a power imbalance accompanies any inclusive practice; whilst it is often 'altruistic and well-meaning' (2009, p. 42), hegemonic forces control the narrative. In relation to education, she cites the neo-liberal agenda increasingly promoted by governments worldwide, critically highlighting how within a seemingly emancipatory approach (e.g. Early Childhood Education) which is inclusive to all, the dominant agenda is one of economics. Thus, Dunne (2009) argues, inclusion will only become a priority to further this agenda on a national level. It might be argued then that as an example of the individualism that Rogoff (2003) critiques, the true inclusion outlined in her own philosophy is far from reality within at least the Global North.

In relation to decolonisation, models of outdoor education have come under scrutiny due to the prevalence of ideas and assumptions coming from the Global North: researchers in this field argue that attention must indeed be paid to the views concerning children's relationship with nature in non-Western societies. Writing from the context of North America, Nxumalo and Cedillo (2017) are concerned about the proliferation of environmental programmes in Early Childhood settings such as those described in this chapter, describing the intention behind these as 'idealised and romanticised' (2017, p. 99), reinforcing assumptions of the child's relationship with nature as pure – that is, above culture. They also identify the problem of viewing children as separate from nature. These notions, according to the authors, are to be contested not least in the light of the colonial and anti-black discourse that they perceive currently pervades North American attitudes. In this respect, as I suggest to students in my own practice, it might be considered that outdoor learning experiences promote a relationship of 'children and nature' as opposed to 'children' and 'nature.'

As indicated above, Nxumalo and Cedillo (2017) argue that assumptions cannot be made about a young child's relationship with nature without considering an ontological position. The child in their own identity forms their relationship with nature. The authors suggest that an onto-epistemology underpinning outdoor education must be an expression of the culture: it should be reflective of Indigenous perspectives and expressive of Indigenous stories, practices and knowledges. For example, they posit that an Early Childhood pedagogy that signifies the role of history, ancestors and spirituality, as well as the ontological connectedness of humans and the environment, might promote a view of the connectedness of all living things, subverting Western dualisms and allowing children the space to 'experience complex relations to the earth, cosmologies, living and non-living beings, and all other matter' (Nxumalo & Cedillo, 2017, p. 103). In turn, they suggest, that through 'interconnectedness comes a responsibility to live in ethical relationality with more-than-human others, where humans are not figured in hierarchical order in relation to others' (Martin, 2007, cited in Nxumalo & Cedillo, 2017, p. 102).

As the discussion moves towards a new chapter, it is important to note that in the light of the ontological underpinning to this book, locating learning within the pre-ontological state of *Dasein* as potentiality-for-Being (Heidegger, 1962), children's experiences of nature might be reflective of their own identities within their own cultures, reflecting their own voices and leading their own learning. This will be given more attention in Chapter Five. However, in closing this penultimate subsection, I provide a final example of inclusion in practice, again from my own personal experience.

Several years ago, I had the privilege of working for a Christian charity in a very multi-cultural area of a large city in the UK, with the remit to establish children's clubs. For one holiday club, which was to be run daily for a week for all children from aged four upwards, the church was not an appropriate setting, therefore it became evident that the sessions should take place at the park. As a neutral space, with the freedom to explore whilst also taking part in organised games, children engaged with each other in a very special way. Several explained how they felt excited to feel unconstrained but safe, and even when it started to rain, and the whole group took shelter under a large tree, the unity within the group was tangible. It seemed that in that moment the racial and religious divisions that seemed to perpetuate within daily experience were in that moment overcome as they connected with the natural environment and each other. Inclusion took place on their terms within this natural space. Later, the children were able to reflect on how this experience enabled them to think differently about themselves as well as themselves in relation to others.

Criticality: models as fixed entities

Finally, critique extends to a consideration of the models explored here as fixed entities: each as an example of what the philosopher Hegel (1977) describes as 'in-itself.' Whilst ESD is not a franchise, it relates closely to the policy documents of the United Nations (e.g. United Nations, 2015; UNESCO, 2020) and based on the notion of three inter-related pillars (Kemp, 2018), practice is grounded on a shared understanding of what the concept entails. Forest School and Eco-Schools respectively, models which exist as internationally recognised enterprises, operate on the basis of buy-in, that is, participants subscribe to an organisation, following which they use generic resources underpinned by specific values and beliefs. Therefore, in light of the ontological premise of this book, some critical commentary on such models of practice is offered.

According to Hegel in *Phenomenology of Spirit* (1977), an entity existing purely in-itself is characterised by a master or lord. The model is the primary subject: an element of determinate contents, which in this case are ecological values and behaviours. But the problem is often that when mastery is made known, there is little acknowledgement of contingency, mediation and context, thereby excluding the element of learning that is relevant and authentic to learners of whatever age. In *Logic* (Hegel, 1975), Hegel's educational process locates truth within rather than external to consciousness. As such, learning (knowledge) is not that which exists beyond the individual, again for example in externally devised models and methods, but that which is deemed as 'self-knowledge in the knowledge of consciousness' (Hegel, 1975, p. 7). What is known as a result of learning is mediated in what is experienced.

In relation to spiritual development, Erricker and Erricker (2000) critique the idea of a one-size-fits-all approach. Albeit primarily evaluating Religious Education, the authors argue against models that perpetuate a particular conceptualisation or representation. Rather, they emphasise 'the importance of the process of pedagogy rather than the inculcation of knowledge' (Erricker & Erricker, 2000, p. 69) and highlight the significance of drawing on the personal and emotional dimension of learning as an example of moving away from these 'fixed points' (71). As their thesis concerns an understanding of spirituality beginning and ending with the human spirit, and considering that any form of knowledge is temporary, Erricker and

Erricker (2000) suggest that when learners gain ownership of their beliefs by self-construction, and when they take responsibility for the creation of meaning in a way that is authentic and meaningful, transformation can occur.

Concluding comments

This chapter has focused on practice in relation to pertinent research, and albeit with a spirit of criticality, has served to highlight how practitioners and researchers in Early Childhood Education might consolidate an understanding of the value of outdoor learning in relation to well-being and social responsibility. Examples from my own experience underline my assertions in this chapter. Acknowledging the requirement to consider context and culture in planning outdoor learning experiences for children, it is more so important that Indigenous voices are heard going forward. In this respect, further research must be undertaken within and with Indigenous communities; I hope therefore that the concerns raised in this chapter might provide some inspiration within the Early Childhood sector. Criticality concerning the fixed nature of some outdoor learning also highlights a limitation, especially when considered in light of the ontological premise of this book. Therefore, in the next chapter, more attention will be paid to pedagogy, with reflections on how this might further inspire a sense of well-being and of responsibility on the part of young children.

References

Bleeksma, E. & Boumann, A. (2024). The exclusion of inclusion: A critical analysis of the use of inclusive language in development practice. *Development in Practice*, 34(1), 92–96. https://doi.org/10.1080/09614524.2023.2272057

Cincera, J., Kroufek, R., Simonova, P., Broukalova, L., Broukal, V. & Skalík, J. (2015). Eco-school in kindergartens: The effects, interpretation, and implementation of a pilot program. *Environmental Education Research*, 23(7), 919–936. https://doi.org/10.1080/13504622.2015.1076768

Cooke, M., Wong, S. & Press, F. (2021). Towards a re-conceptualisation of risk in early childhood education. *Contemporary Issues in Early Childhood*, 22(1), 5–19. https://doi.org/10.1177/1463949119840740

Dunne, L. (2009). Discourses of inclusion: A critique. *Power and Education*, 1(1), 42–56. https://doi.org/10.2304/power.2009.1.1.42

Elliott, S. & Chancellor, B. (2014). From forest preschool to bush kinder: An inspirational approach to preschool provision in Australia. *Australasian Journal of Early Childhood*, 39(4), 45–53. https://doi.org/10.1177/183693911403900407

Else, P. (2009). *The value of play*. London: Continuum International Publishing Group.

Erricker, C. & Erricker, J. (2000). *Reconstructing religious, spiritual and moral education*. London: Routledge Falmer.

Featherbe, A., Lloyd-Evans, L. & Moylett, H. (2023). Developing a culture of sustainability in early childhood education. In C. Nutbrown (Ed.), *Early childhood education: Current realities and future priorities* (pp. 247–259). London: Sage.

Forest School Association. (2024). What is the forest school association? Available from: https://forestschoolassociation.org/the-forest-school-association/

Garden, A. & Downes, G. (2023). A systematic view of forest schools literature in England. *International Journal of Primary, Elementary and Early Years Education*, 51(2), 320–336. https://doi.org/10.1080/03004279.2021.1971275

Gegeo, D. & Watson-Gegeo, K.A. (2001). How we know: Kwara'ae rural villagers doing indigenous epistemology. *The Contemporary Pacific*, 13(1), 55–88.

Gillan, K., Mellor, S. & Krakouer, J. (2017). *The case for urgency: Advocating for indigenous voice in education*. Melbourne: ACER Press.

Grenier, J. & Vollans, C. (2023). *Putting the EYFS curriculum into practice*. London: Sage.

Heidegger, M. (1962). *Being and time*. Oxford: Blackwell Publishers.

Hegel, G. (1975). *Hegel's logic*. Oxford: Clarendon Press.

Hegel, G. (1977). *Phenomenology of spirit*. Oxford: Oxford University Press.

Kemp, N. (2018). Early childhood education for sustainability. In S. Powell & K. Smith (Eds.), *An introduction to early childhood studies* (pp. 247–259). Los Angeles: Sage.

Knight, S. (2016). *Forest school in practice*. London: Sage.

Korkmaz, A. & Yildiz, T.G. (2017). Assessing preschools using the Eco-Schools program in terms of educating for sustainable development in early childhood education. *European Early Childhood Education Research Journal*, 25(4), 595–611. https://10.1080/1350293X.2017.1331074

Nikiforidou, Z., Lavin-Miles, Z. & Luff, P. (2020). Bat conservation in the foundation stage. In P. Bamber (Ed.), *Teacher education for sustainable development and global citizenship* (pp. 113–121). Abingdon: Routledge.

Nxumalo, F. & Cedillo, S. (2017). Decolonizing place in early childhood studies: Thinking with Indigenous onto-epistemologies and Black feminist geographies. *Global Studies of Childhood*, 7(2), 99–112. https://doi.org/10.1177/2043610617703831

Pramling Samuelsson, I. (2011). Why we should begin early with ESD: The role of early childhood education. *International Journal of Early Childhood*, 43, 103–118. https://doi.org/10.1007/s13158-011-0034-x

Robinson, C. (2019). Young children's spirituality: A focus on engaging with nature. *Australasian Journal of Early Childhood*, 44(4), 339–350. https://doi.org/10.1177/1836939119870907

Rogoff, B. (2003). *The cultural nature of human development*. Oxford: Oxford University Press.

Rogoff, B. & Mejía-Arauz, R. (2022). The key role of community in Learning by Observing and Pitching In to family and community endeavours. *Journal for the Study of Education and Development*, 45(3), 494–548. https://doi.org/10.1080/02103702.2022.2086770

United Nations. (1989). *Convention on the rights of the child*. London: Unicef.

United Nations. (2015). *The UN sustainable development goals*. Available from: http://www.un.org/sustainabledevelopment/summit/

United Nations Educational, Scientific and Cultural Organisation [UNESCO]. (2020). *Education for sustainable development: A roadmap*. Paris: UNESCO. https://doi.org/10.54675/YFRE1448

Williams-Siegfredsen, J. (2017). *Understanding the Danish forest school approach: Early years education in practice*. 2nd ed. London: Routledge. https://doi.org/10.4324/9781315542027

Wills, R. (2021). A philosophical perspective on provision for cultural development in an English context. In R. Wills, M. de Souza, J. Mata-McMahon, M. Abu Bakar & C. Roux (Eds.), *The Bloomsbury handbook of culture and identity from early childhood to early adulthood* (pp. 197–208). London: Bloomsbury Academic.

Wilson, E.O. (1984). *Biophilia*. Cambridge, Massachusetts & London: Harvard University Press.

World Commission on Environment and Development [WCED]. (1987). *Our common future*. Oxford: Oxford University Press.

Yarwood, R. & Tyrell, N. (2012). Why children's geographies? *Geography*, 97(3), 123–128.

5 Children's spirituality, nature and pedagogy

Introduction

At this point of the discussion, it is necessary to explore, from the foundational understanding of the spiritual nature of outdoor experience and its benefits for young children's learning and development, how a spiritual pedagogy might progress from the ontological starting point of innate spirituality to positive social action. Within the understandings of children's spirituality and nature already addressed, this chapter will propose a pedagogical process that allows learners to draw on the sense of personal and social well-being that nature inspires, to take responsibility, and engage in positive behaviours that promote sustainability. As such, spiritual awareness should not only be an experience 'in-itself' (Hegel, 1977) but become manifest in action.

Being and potentiality-for-Being

As stated in Chapter Two, a belief in the innate and universal state of spirituality has its roots in ontology. For this discussion, the work of Heidegger (1962, 1978) has provided a philosophical underpinning throughout this book; it is relevant here to the notion of spirituality as the *a priori* dimension in children's lives that is the starting point for spiritual awareness and the development of identity and connectedness. However, Heidegger's philosophical position concerns not just ontology but pre-ontology. *Dasein*, the ontological state (Heidegger, 1962, p. 32) which etymologically means 'being there' (27), is a manner of Being. It is the state of Being that exists before one recognises oneself or is recognised as an entity. However, prior to *Dasein* is essence; this is a universal phenomenon and has no definition. Hence, prior to immersion in the world, Being is a pure and uncompromised pre-ontological state which, it might be argued, exists even before spirituality.

From this essential state, *Dasein* reveals how essence 'is.' As primordial, it is still prior to the understanding of the self as an entity; *Dasein* pertains to the possibility of what the self can become in one's Being (Heidegger, 1962). Truth is the truth of what is learnt through Being. In relation to this, it might be suggested therefore that spiritual pedagogy, with its ontological foundation,

DOI: 10.4324/9781003483939-6

Children's spirituality, nature and pedagogy 71

might be considered a pedagogy of possibility, with the Being of the child as the starting point for a mode of education in which they become transparent in their own Being. In colloquial terms, the child's essence is a blank canvas from which *Dasein* issues forth its potentialities. Thus, such learning involves the projection of one's potentiality into the making of meaning.

Acknowledging *Dasein's* potentiality-for-Being, learning is thus revealed authentically through 'care.' This state of Being is self-projective, and when *Dasein* is 'ahead of itself in care,' learners in their Being become authentic to their own potentiality (Heidegger, 1962, p. 236). This represents the continuation of the learner's own potentiality, ahead of itself and embracing an awareness of what is being learnt. When this awareness 'stands out' in what Heidegger calls the 'ecstatic,' the self can make meaning drawn from its own potentiality and make a response (Heidegger, 1978, p. 241).

This then is the platform for the possibility of inhered truth (Heidegger, 1978, p. 229), through which children evaluate their place in the world in the light of their own Being, and respond to the situations they find themselves in. The outcome is undefined and often unknown; nevertheless, as the student is brought towards Being ahead of themselves in care, manifestations of this learning become apparent. When the child responds personally to learning, amazing things can happen. This also has implications for the role of the teacher: when the teacher's own *Dasein* allows for the realisation of the *Dasein* of the students, change can ensue. According to Tubbs (2005), the teacher who allows students to learn learning itself as it unfolds 'its own most power for disclosing the essence of all things' (Tubbs, 2005, p. 133), is spiritual.

This philosophy has resonance for young children learning in nature when pedagogy is drawn on the learner's own self-discovery, based on a recognition of the awareness that affords meaning to open-ended situations. When the authentic self is the starting point for each activity, whether planned or free-flow, experiences such as creating an imaginary fire, noticing clouds and birds, sitting in stillness or climbing a tree can be how children come to understand who they are in relation to the world, what they are capable of, and who they might become. These examples are small yet significant ways of empowering the 'deeply felt impulse that is the innate spirituality of children' (Hart, 2003, p. 173), which allows educators 'to let their authentic or spiritual voices be heard' (Bosacki, 2001, p. 163). Here the authentic learner does not look outside of Being for its truth. The truth of meaning begins and ends with the Being that learns its own truth.

Webster (2018) draws parallels between the understanding of spirituality as Being, and the work of John Dewey. Dewey's democratic approach to education espouses a child-centred, experiential pedagogy, aiming to meet social needs and promote self-development. As such, he considers education as a means of inspiring a moral and spiritual way of life (Wang, 2016 cited in Webster, 2018).

Webster identifies Dewey's notion of the 'being' mode of existence as akin to his own view of innate children's spirituality, and rather than 'having' spirituality in a pre-determined form to be consumed (such as a religious framework), for Webster, after Dewey, being spiritual concerns the development of the inner person, promoting virtuous behaviours such as being 'accepting, tolerant and loving' (Webster, 2018, p. 76).

The idea of potentiality is also evident in Dewey's ideas, and as Webster points out, the ontological is prioritised over the epistemological. Rather than acquiring prescribed information through a pre-determined curriculum, it is the 'internal energy' of spirit as a constituent of self that inspires authentic learning within which the learner is personally invested. Webster (2018) notes that similar to Heidegger, Dewey considers spirituality existentially. The basis for education is not to gain objective truth, but to consider who one is, what one should do and 'how one ought to live' (Webster, 2018, p. 80). Reflective of Heideggerian terms, in this respect, children can make meaning drawn from their own potentiality-for-Being (Heidegger, 1962).

Making meaning and interpreting meaning in the light of experience are key aspects of Dewey's philosophy that take us further than that of the pioneers introduced in Chapter Three. Dewey does not understand meaning in the sense of facts or head-knowledge. His idea of 'knowing' is more akin to a resonance than the actualisation of concepts and ideas, and as he points out in *Experience and Nature* (2008), the qualities of intuition, sense, feelings and perception that contribute to spiritual learning exist in a dimension other than thought consciousness (Dewey, 2008, p. 235). Thus, whereas the mind involves 'a whole system of meanings' (229), experiential learning is concerned more with awareness or the perception of meanings. These meanings are for the here and now; they might be intermittent, vague and not necessarily actualised in language (230). Nevertheless, they are important to young learners and do have meaning even though this might not be articulated or easily expressed.

Dewey's notion of experience is also explored in his text *Art as Experience* (1934). In a similar vein to his view of meaning, 'experience' here is holistic. He aims to avoid the individualising and self-sufficient rhetoric of 'an' experience, focusing rather on how authentic learning might become manifest through the connection of a variety of events in a movement of flow between individuals and environments. This involves engagement with materials and processes, but also involves the unfolding of ideas. It then prioritises the progression of the learning experience, from the aesthetic moment through to the integration of meaning. It is therefore the process of learning that has significance – not the end result. In *Democracy and Education* (2012), Dewey states the aims of education. Simply, education is the continued capacity for growth. His growth principle articulates the idea of learning as a continuous present. This suggests that learning and growing continue throughout a child's life and experience. Growth is emotional and moral as well as intellectual. It concerns liberation and enrichment, and promotes deep and authentic understanding (Heilbronn, 2018). This idea, reminiscent of the philosophy of Froebel explored in Chapter Two, with the image of children as seedlings to be nurtured within enabling environments, is also reflected in the Reggio Emilia approach – the constructivist view of education established by Loris Malaguzzi in Italy in the period following the second world war (Edwards et al., 1993). According to Malaguzzi, children have agency. Education, within appropriate environments, allows for the personal growth of all children. Equally, again akin to the Froebelian approach, children must be able to learn through experiences of touching, moving, listening and observing in relation to other children and with material items in the world. It is essential that learners are allowed to explore objects, places and spaces, have some control over the direction of their learning and be afforded endless ways and opportunities to express themselves (Edwards et al., 1993).

As noted in previous chapters, the outdoor space can act as an affordance for such expression. In relation to outdoor learning, at least for the youngest children in my own school and as stated in an earlier chapter, the environment acts as an egalitarian provider of educational experience. Each child, whether they have special educational needs or disabilities, have English as a second language, are advanced in their academic development or are simply at the expected level, can access nature in a way that is relevant to them on their own terms. At 'The Lodge' children frequently ask: 'please can we,' suggesting that children have their own ideas for imaginary play and creativity such as engaging in role play in the mud kitchen, or for physical activity as they create an obstacle course using tyres, pallets and other natural resources. Other children simply lose themselves in their own worlds of adventure or reflection, sitting in the quiet area and reading, and others create running games with rules that the teachers need to 'referee.' With very little input from staff, each child makes meaning based on their own experiences, and as much as teachers observe aspects of learning and development, nothing is measured or assessed.

The ideas of potentiality-for-Being (Heidegger, 1962) and democracy (Dewey, 2008) as explored here, are also evident within contemporary policy. As outlined in Chapter One, within *Belonging, Being and Becoming: The Early Years Learning Framework for Australia* (Australian Government Department of Education, 2022), supporting children in their Being – in the here and now – is deemed as important as who they will become in the future. This policy is underlined by an understanding that children of all ages can develop their own identities within their own communities. Family and community are recognised as the first educators, and in particular, culture is linked to existence. In response to play-based and place-based programmes and activities, children are empowered to be agents in learning, and as they develop and learn, they can construct their own understandings of the world and respond in a way that 'enables active citizenship' (Australian Government Department of Education, 2022, p. 6).

New Zealand's *Early Learning Curriculum Framework* (New Zealand Ministry for Education, 2023), promotes the idea that all children, regardless of background, are entitled to equitable access to learning that affirms their identity and encourages positive relationships with others. They are given opportunities to express themselves through creativity and in the light of their own traditions, values and stories, can communicate their ideas and feelings in expressive ways. Meanwhile, albeit open to critique, democracy is also evident in the *Early Years Foundation Stage Statutory Framework* (DfE, 2023) for Early Childhood Education in England. In this policy, young children are encouraged to engage with the environment, explore and think critically, ask how and why, relate to others and solve problems. This framework additionally encourages active learning based on interests, with questioning and curiosity leading the learning (DfE, 2023).

As stated in Chapter One, each country represented here has guidance concerning outdoor learning, and in the case of Australia and New Zealand, the significance of developing young children's relationship with nature for well-being and spiritual development is noted. Therefore, whilst the views of Heidegger, Dewey and Malaguzzi span a century of educational theory and practice, their influence is still evident today, and each one offers something valuable to the development of a spiritual pedagogy for contemporary Early Childhood Education. To continue, the discussion now turns to critical pedagogy.

Critical Pedagogy

Paulo Freire, a twentieth century Brazilian educator and philosopher, is considered as a foundational voice in the arena of Critical Pedagogy. In his seminal text *Pedagogy of the Oppressed* (1970/1993), he argues for personal freedom in learning, with the intention that education promotes transformation. Reacting to his own cultural situation of struggle in the developing world following the economic crisis of 1929, and then the Second World War, he offered a creative approach to encouraging and empowering those oppressed by a culture of silence. He offered a way for these individuals and groups to critically respond to the culture forced on them, to aim for liberation. Education was considered as one of the instruments of domination, therefore through his Critical Pedagogy, learners were encouraged to no longer be recipients of the knowledge and understandings of teachers, engaging in a pre-determined linear learning process, but agents of their own learning, participating with others and engaging in 'reflection and action upon the world in order to transform it' (Freire, 1993, p. 33).

There are similarities here with the Heideggerian and Deweyan views of learning as described above. Freire begins his text (1993) suggesting that humanisation, or liberation, is an ontological possibility. Through critical recognition and reflection on the structures, people and practices that oppress, this possibility can be realised through transforming actions that create new situations. Such reflection and action 'makes possible the pursuit of a fuller humanity' (Freire, 1993, p. 29). Akin to Heidegger's notion of care (Heidegger, 1962) the individual takes part in their own education, drawing on their ontological possibilities to become actors in their own transformation. Also, Freire acknowledges that no people are separated from culture, and that when an oppressive objective social reality is accepted as normative, such societal beliefs and behaviours are adopted within the collective consciousness (Freire, 1993). However, through Critical Pedagogy, they can strive to be free in their being. Referring very briefly again to Heidegger (1962), this does not concern Being for another, which involves a dualistic positing of self and other which inevitably excludes but considers what it means to be fully human as Being-in-the-world.

Drawing parallels also with Dewey, from this ontological starting point, Freire's ideas concerning education go beyond the teaching of knowledge as facts in what he critically terms the 'banking concept' (Freire, 1993, p. 53). Contrary to the 'banking concept,' Freire promotes creativity, enquiry, free thinking and co-operation. Learning lies not only within cognition but within consciousness. As noted earlier in the literature of children's spirituality, spiritual learning resides within a meta-consciousness which, often bypassing fixed ideas or thoughts, connects both inner and outer human dimensions for authentic learning (Hay & Nye, 2006). However, for Freire (1993), education is also about having consciousness of consciousness. This offers a critical approach to learning, within which students become aware of the limitations of the deposit-making aspects of knowledge and are able rather to engage in questioning and reflecting within what he terms 'problem-posing education' (Freire, 1993, p. 60). This places the responsibility for discovering and understanding new knowledge onto the learner or learners and, based on the view that learning is constantly reformed and re-evaluated through each instance of reflection, learning does not become fixed but is always relevant to each instance, culture and time, and open to revision. Rather than a linear approach, as in the performative banking concept, but also rather than the liberationist approach of Heidegger and Dewey, Freire's notion of children having consciousness of consciousness suggests a more dialectical process of learning.

Before moving on from Freire, the significance of this approach in outdoor learning is illustrated. Again, when outside at 'The Lodge,' another question frequently asked is 'can you watch me' or similarly, 'can you see what we have done?' Through the children's play and creativity, undertaken as suggested earlier on their own terms, young children at my school are often eager to explain to staff how they have come to (for example) tell a story through role play or create scenery from natural objects – the end result of a process of discussion, debate and evaluation, and often, disagreement. This is problem-posing education in action! In terms of awareness, it is also frequently evident how children feel different outdoors. They relish a rainy day as they love to get wet, expressing how it makes them feel tingly, and as they get dirty in mud, they exclaim how it is funny to slip and slide in their wellies. On a sunny day they explain how the warmth creates happiness, and when they return inside after a session in the bitter cold, it makes them feel snuggly and safe. Through this sensorial awareness, not only do children become aware of their own feelings in relation to their bodies, but also express something of their symbiotic relationship with nature – they want to be kind to the earth as it is kind to them.

Freire's ideas as highlighted here are reminiscent of Hegel's philosophy, briefly introduced in Chapter Four. This is again relevant to the current discussion in relation to how learners learn learning in the light of their own contingency, that is, the development of their identity within culture, and it also concerns the relationship of learning and the learner with respect to the structures within which education takes place, in this context, Early Childhood Education. Additionally, Hegel's philosophy sheds light on how children might yet learn authentically whilst still experiencing their education within a burgeoning paradigm of performativity.

Hegel's dialectic (1977) concerns a relationship of struggle between two forms of consciousness. Again as introduced in Chapter Four, the master, characterised as a Stoic, represents objectivity – knowledge 'in-itself.' This is knowledge which is 'as it is' – objective, universal and pure. As an entity in-itself it adopts the upper hand in learning and sets the standard against which knowledge is understood. However, Hegel notes that a universal cannot be known if it is a thing in-itself: it merely amounts to nothingness, devoid of the personal content that makes learning meaningful. Learners do not exist apart from the world, therefore there must always be another form of consciousness that is 'for us,' or subjective.

Hegel (1977) characterises this consciousness as a slave: not in-itself but for-itself: the natural self-consciousness or individual who strives for self-actualisation through gaining knowledge on their own terms. They are the element for which free self-consciousness comes to know itself in the many and varied forms of life as the negativity of the universal. In the search for subjective and individual knowledge, the slave attempts liberation from the universal. This movement symbolises the ontological philosophy of Heidegger (1962) or the democratic pedagogy of Dewey (2008).

Yet the interesting element of this dialectical illustration is that whilst each character attempts alienation from the other in their bid for freedom, it is the recognition of their need for each other for life that is educative. The truth of the master comes in his dependence on the slave. He is a master because he has a slave. He needs the negativity of himself to establish his position. As Hegel (1977, p. 116) writes: 'He achieves his recognition through another

Children's spirituality, nature and pedagogy 77

consciousness.' Characterised as the 'Unhappy Consciousness,' a movement of negation continues. Through this, each comes to understand that in seeking the negation of the other, the self only has real meaning when recognised in relation to the other. Therefore, neither should have the upper hand. This, as noted in relation to Freire (1993), is when learners develop consciousness of consciousness.

From the starting point of ontological (spiritual) awareness and the personal meaning that can be made in response to this, it is the realisation of the significance of the relation of the two forms of consciousness that, according to Rose (1992), is educative. Thought consciousness realises what might previously have been a sense or feeling and allows for the critical questioning and problem-solving that moving forward will make a difference, both to learners and their relationships, but also the world. This now identifies a significant point in the discussion concerning how children's experiences of nature move from nurturing spirituality and well-being to the development of values and behaviours that promote sustainability.

However it is important to point out before concluding this sub-section, and in the light of the critique of models and methods as presented in Chapter Four, that Hegel's dialectic (1977) itself might be perceived as validating the practices of oppressors as entities of mastery, and much has been written about this. For example, Hegel has been accused of perpetuating a colonial stance, thus advocating racism through the exclusion of the 'other' from being (Fanon, 1952, cited in Ogungbure, 2018). Nevertheless, it is my assertion that the continuation of negation through the Unhappy Consciousness offers a process of learning which ensures that learning is always personal, relational and responsive to human experience. Therefore, as with Freire (1993), a dialectical approach to education ensures that learning makes a difference to people within communities, be they local or global, and inspires change.

Bildung: a proposed process of learning for spirituality and nature in Early Childhood Education

Within my own pedagogical perspective, learning is considered as a process, which as stated above, is personal, continuous and transformative. I consider each lesson within the Early Childhood paradigm as an event which has an impact on the lived experience of children as individuals and within communities. From an ontological starting point of potentiality, learning is therefore spiritual, drawing on children's innate sensibilities and possibilities, afforded by experiences and engagement within enabling environments, including awareness sensing, creating, wondering and reflecting, and leading to transformation. As such, it is reflective of the philosophical perspectives presented here.

78 *Children's spirituality, nature and pedagogy*

However, it is also important to note, in line with the detail concerning Hegelian thought, that for many across the globe, Early Childhood Education is framed by policy, much of which, as stated earlier, does not make explicit reference to spirituality. As much as performative directives from governments, as external drivers of education, are in many cases critiqued by scholars (for example, Adams et al., 2016) and practitioners, it is nevertheless impossible to overcome these influences on teaching and learning. Also, as Hegel (1977) suggests and has already been pointed out, some child-centred approaches to Early Childhood Education and outdoor learning are themselves open to critique in the light of non-Western voices and perspectives.

Furthermore, there is an ethical dilemma inherent in a mode of education in which individuals, contingent in their Being (Heidegger, 1962), establish the foundation for their education without similar critique. Whilst for Heidegger, Being is intrinsic to the process of coming to 'know,' it must be acknowledged also that in his philosophy Being *is* the truth. As such it contains the possibility of allowing for the acceptance of meanings that might be unhelpful or unkind. Therefore again, a dialectical philosophical perspective is helpful since through critique, reflection and problem-solving, children not only lead their own learning but within a dialectical relationship with the curriculum and beliefs and values of the school, engage in a continuous process of meaning-making and action. Furthermore, when spiritual awareness, inspired by children's innate spirituality, is brought to thought consciousness, learners can then act on the significance of this awareness. In this respect, the awareness does not exist merely as an experience 'in-itself,' but has significance for the lived present and future of others, much like the aspirations for sustainability outlined in the Brundtland report (WCED, 1987) introduced in Chapter Four.

The dialectical approach then provides a rationale for the inclusion of spirituality in the policies and practices of Early Childhood Education. Being neither an expression of 'in-itself' for example in relation to religion or any other form of dogma, nor entirely person-centred (or indeed pertaining to an unclear understanding of spirituality that might make some teachers feel uneasy), the relationship between the two forms of consciousness and the interaction between them offer a process of learning that can be meaningful to both children's spirituality within their own identities and contexts, but also the means by which this might be understood within the existing curriculum.

My own perspective on learning is influenced by 'Bildung,' drawn from the idea of German educator Wilhelm von Humboldt (1767–1835) who proposes this process as the personal development of the individual into Being and within temporality (von Humboldt, 2000). Actions of the individual involve an interaction with others, in this case named 'world' and as Nordenbo (2003) outlines, the interaction reflects the action of taking a photograph – with 'bild' meaning 'image' and the suffix 'ung' representing the process. As von Humboldt (2000, p. 58) writes, between self and other is 'the most general, most animated and most unrestrained interplay,' with the possibility of learning arising from what occurs during the interplay.

Learners in their own contingency, or in this case, on the basis of their innate spirituality, reach out beyond themselves to experience the world through relationships and activities. Such experiences might promote spiritual awareness through the hallmarks of spirituality – or in the language of Kirmani and Kirmani (2009), sensitivities; but importantly, following this, there is a process of reflection and meaning-making as learners process 'that which (he) undertakes outside himself' (von Humboldt, 2000, p. 59). As with Dewey (2008), learning involves the senses, and as with Heidegger (1962), learning is open-ended, with no experience being the same. But also in line with Freire (1993) and Hegel (1977), the interplay ensures that neither the individual nor the 'world' become examples of 'in-itself' but the value of each lies in its relation to the other. Like the movement of the Unhappy Consciousness (Hegel, 1977), Bildung's interplay between self and other is a continuous movement (von Humboldt, 2000).

Putting my own process of learning into practice in relation to nature and spirituality, it is my belief that before children access the outdoor learning environment, their Being as *Dasein*, contains the possibility of how they will respond to their experiences. Next, they are led from this *a priori* state to gain awareness of their Being through their reaching out to the world – the interplay of self with other. As illustrated throughout this book, a child might experience presence or stillness through careful observation, counting, noticing, drawing or thinking. They might engage in imaginative play or creativity through role play, natural art, digging or building. A sense of wonder might be awakened when the sun peeps out from behind a cloud, rain suddenly makes the grass muddy or the sound of an aeroplane or birds on a cloudy day indicate a life beyond what can be seen. Children can engage in individual or collective play, learning how to experiment or to extend their skills as well as discuss, negotiate, share and support each other. Their senses and bodily (corporeal) experiences connect with their emotions and imagination and whilst awareness might bypass cognition at this point, the children experience what is described by Dewey (2008) as a resonance where the qualities of intuition, sense, feelings and perception are the primary modes of learning.

Nevertheless, as the process continues, the interplay involves a return to thought consciousness as learning begins to include evaluation. In this next phase, awareness sensing and thought consciousness engage in a dialectical manner so that the learning can be recognised and understood. This is not a retrieving of information back to thought consciousness as in a linear or didactic form of learning, but an interpretation of events as a mode of potentiality; learning still has an ontological foundation but awareness is brought into the realm of understanding, simply asking: what does this mean? This part of the process involves rumination and meaning-making, as well as problem solving and critical reflection. In the open-ended outdoor environment, as noted above, freedom in learning includes the opportunity to critically appraise the world in order to transform it. It is at this point that children try to make sense of their experiences and come up with their own questions, and sometimes answers. These questions might relate to immediate issues such as how to keep the space tidy, or how to work together as a team. But often the questions relate to how they might draw on their concerns for others and the world.

Therefore, the next step is that learning is made manifest in care. From the ontological state of possibility, through interplay with the environment to promote awareness, back to thought consciousness to make meaning, and now again reaching outwards from the self, children must be able to offer a response. This can lead, for example, to their taking responsibility in ways such as protecting creatures like bugs and local wildlife, or the natural environment itself through, for example, watering and litter-picking. It might also allow children to become cognisant of an enhanced sense of self in relation to others in the world, leading to egalitarian expressions of friendship towards all children. It might concern children's care for pets or other domestic creatures, but also promote a concern for the future of the world, encouraging them to take part in responsible sustainable actions.

Through learning in nature or the outdoor space, young children have the potential to become empowered to make a difference in the world. And as the process of 'Bildung' is continual, spiritual education also does not end. It becomes a continuous stream of reflection and action, constantly inspiring change. Therefore the possibility is endless. It is hoped that learning will continue through our children's lives, through different stages of maturity, so they might be in the future, responsible adult citizens. Our mandate as scholars and practitioners then is to inspire agency; as we engage in our own spiritual education, influencing policy and practice, as well as allowing for the potentiality of our students, we too can become agents for personal, spiritual and political change.

Concluding comments

Underpinned by the pedagogical positions of the theorists introduced in this chapter, the discussion has moved from highlighting how young children's spirituality, albeit not always explicit within Early Childhood policy but certainly evident through young children's experiences in nature, through their awareness and relationship with the world, might be the starting point for care and responsibility. Whilst critiquing but not negating the current paradigm of education for young children across many contexts globally, it is suggested, based on the various aspects of this book, that not only is it important for learners that policy revisions in the future start to include the language of spirituality, but that it is an understanding of children's potentiality that might allow for meaningful learning, leading to transformation – both on the part of the children themselves as authentic learners, and for their communities, both local and global. Suggestions for implementation and ideas for policy makers and practitioners are thus provided in the brief final chapter.

References

Adams, K., Bull, L. & Maynes, M.L. (2016). Towards an understanding of the distinctive features of young children's spirituality. *European Early Childhood Education Research Journal*, 24(5), 760–774. https://doi.org/10.1080/1350293X.2014.996425

Australian Government Department of Education. (2022). *Belonging, being and becoming: The early years learning framework for Australia* [EYLF] (V2.0). ACT: Australian Government Department of Education for the Ministerial Council. Available from: https://www.acecqa.gov.au/sites/default/files/2023-01/EYLF-2022-V2.0.pdf

Bosacki, S. (2001). Theory of mind or theory of soul? The role of spirituality in children's understanding of mind and emotions. In C. Erricker, J. Erricker & C. Ota (Eds.), *Spiritual education: New perspectives for the 21st century* (pp. 156–169). Brighton: Sussex Academic Press.

Department for Education. (2023). *Early years foundation stage statutory framework*. Available from: https://assets.publishing.service.gov.uk/media/65aa5e42ed27ca0 01327b2c7/EYFS_statutory_framework_for_group_and_school_based_providers .pdf

Dewey, J. (1934). *Art as experience*. New York: Minton, Balch and Company.

Dewey, J. (2008). *Experience and nature*. Carbondale: Southern Illinois University Press.

Dewey, J. (2012). *Democracy and education*. Dayboro: Emereo Publishing.

Edwards, C., Gandini, L. & Forman, G. (1993). Introduction: Background and starting points. In C. Edwards, L. Gandini & G. Forman (Eds.), *The hundred languages of children: The Reggio Emilia approach to early childhood* (pp. 5–26). Norwood, NJ: Ablex Publishing Corporation.

Freire, P. (1993). *Pedagogy of the oppressed*. London: Penguin Classics.

Hart, T. (2003). *The secret spiritual world of children*. Makawao: Inner Ocean Publishing.

Hay, D. & Nye, R. (2006). *The spirit of the child*. London: Jessica Kingsley Publishers.

Hegel, G. (1977). *Phenomenology of spirit*. Oxford: Oxford University Press.

Heidegger, M. (1962). *Being and time*. Oxford: Blackwell Publishers.

Heidegger, M. (1978). Letter on humanism. In M. Heidegger, *Basic writings*. London: Routledge.

Heilbronn, R. (2018) Growth and growing in education: Dewey's relevance to current Malaise. *Journal of Philosophy of Education*, 52(2), 301–315. https://doi.org/10 .1111/1467-9752.12287

Kirmani, M.H. & Kirmani, S. (2009). Recognition of seven spiritual identities and its implications on children. *International Journal of Children's Spirituality*, 14(4), 369–383. https://doi.org/10.1080/13644360903293630

New Zealand Ministry for Education. (2023). Early learning *curriculum framework. He Anga Marau Kohungahunga*. Available from: https://assets.education.govt.nz /public/Documents/News/News-2023/Early-Learning-Curriculum-Framework -2023.pdf

Nordenbo, S.E. (2003). Bildung and the thinking of Bildung. In L. Lovlie, K. P. Mortensen & S. E. Nordenbo (Eds.), *Educating humanity. Bildung in postmodernity* (pp. 25–36). Oxford: Blackwell Publishing.

Ogungbure, A.A. (2018). Dialectics of oppression: Fanon's Anti-colonial critique of Hegel's Dialectics. *Africology: The Journal of Pan African Studies*, 12(7), 216–230. Available from: https://jpanafrican.org/docs/vol12no7/12.7-12-Ogungbure-final.pdf

Rose, G. (1992). *The broken middle*. Oxford: Blackwell Publishers.

Tubbs, N. (2005). *The philosophy of the teacher*. Oxford: Blackwell Publishing.

von Humboldt, W. (2000). Theory of Bildung. In I. Westbury, S. Hopmann & K. Riquarts (Eds.), *Teaching as a reflective practice* (pp. 57–61). London: Lawrence Erlbaum.

Webster, R.S. (2018). Being spiritually educated. In M. de Souza & A. Halafoff (Eds.), *Re-Enchanting education and spiritual wellbeing* (pp. 73–85). London: Routledge.

World Commission on Environment and Development [WCED]. (1987). *Our common future*. Oxford: Oxford University Press.

6 Children's spirituality and nature
Recommendations for policy and practice

Introduction

This book is aimed at policy makers in Early Childhood Education, with a view to highlighting the problem arising from the deficiency of the rhetoric of spirituality in policy, and to highlight the benefits of exploring an understanding of spirituality and outdoor learning for the development of children's well-being. Furthermore, as has been noted, spiritual development might extend further than a child's own sense of self, and it is also suggested in this text that their spiritual awareness, brought to consciousness through reflection and rumination, can inspire positive responses towards the world, including support for environmental issues. This text is also aimed at Early Childhood practitioners and leaders who must manage the tension between the changing priorities in education and understanding the benefits of learning outdoors, to provide encouragement and support spiritual awareness within the curriculum alongside a more formal approach. In closing this discussion, I offer recommendations for future work.

The book will additionally be of relevance to researchers within the field of Early Childhood Education and Care. Whilst the benefits of young children learning outdoors are reflected in relevant literature, the role of spirituality is less well represented, with the most significant articles and chapters already cited in this publication. Therefore, ideas for future research are also suggested, hoping that the issue of children's spirituality and nature will be an ongoing conversation resulting in developments in both understanding and practice.

Policy and practice

At a time when environmental concerns and mental health issues seem to dominate political and media-driven conversations, Early Childhood Education, which historically has prioritised engagement with nature and well-being through a child-centred pedagogy, is in many countries across the globe now experiencing a move towards a more technocratic paradigm of education. From my own experience as a practitioner, I have first-hand knowledge of how learning outdoors, albeit wonderful (illustrated in the vignettes of the Preamble and examples provided throughout this book), is often deemed to be the treat for a Friday afternoon, or the activities children do when they have finished their more formal learning. When once children in pre-school and the first year of school were offered outdoor learning at all times of the day within an integrated curriculum design, a more subject-driven approach now means that time outdoors is timetabled rather than considered a valuable experience connected to all areas of learning.

Therefore, my first recommendation for policy makers is that in future revisions of documentation, ministers for Education, or leaders in Early Childhood Education might again consider learning outdoors as a full-time provision. Reflecting the essence of Loris Malaguzzi, for whom the environment serves as a 'third educator' (1994, cited in Gandini, 1993), and in light of the positive experiences described in this book, I suggest that during the foundational years of education for young children, the personal and emotional development, including the physical and relational, that takes place when children are free to explore, be creative or problem-solve in the outdoor space, will reap benefits for the future. Young children's learning of learning (Tubbs, 2005), which can occur spontaneously as they access the egalitarian outdoor space, will inspire them to be independent and self-assured, whilst inclusive of others; thus, it might enable children to be 'school-ready' as much, if not more so, than the approach that prioritises planning and progression of knowledge and skills.

In the light of this, my recommendation for leaders and teachers is that the outdoor space is utilised as a physical and conceptual classroom. Phonics, Science, Art, Music, Writing and other curriculum areas can be undertaken outside. As much as a more formal pedagogy in some cases must be applied, the benefits of (for example) walking whilst learning, looking for things, comparing and contrasting, and recording not only support physical and social development as well as knowledge and skills, but as suggested by one young child, aged four – they just learn better. Furthermore, as stated in Chapter Four, we might not consider the outdoor space as a dualistic opposite to the classroom, but it could become a learning partner which promotes children's engagement with nature, so they might be 'children in nature' rather than 'children' in 'nature.'

Conceptually, as Eaude (2020) suggests, and similar to the meta-spaces of spirituality presented through the work of Goodliff (2016) in Chapter Two, the non-physical spaces created through play, creativity and wider curriculum areas might become the nexus of identities, cultures, values and beliefs, and trusting relationships, and the mode through which the power differential of teacher and learner might be redressed to acknowledge all as learners. Furthermore, within such safe conceptual spaces which promote belonging, children can find their voice; as agents of learning, they can challenge assumptions and offer a vision for the future (Eaude, 2020). As such, it is the existential dimension of education that is highlighted here, and, bringing the discussion back to Heidegger (1962) and the notion of Being, it concerns who children are in their existence and how they will develop in their potentiality-for-Being.

Concerning children's spirituality, it is noted here that the absence of rhetoric and language pertaining to this essential human dimension in policy in some contexts is a deficit. For countries that prioritise spirituality, even so, there is some lack of understanding concerning how to implement spiritual development within the curriculum, for example in Australia (Robinson, 2019); nevertheless for others, such as Canada and New Zealand, it is more comfortably embedded in the Early Childhood curriculum. It is hoped that through the illustrations and exploration of themes in this book, particularly in the light of the proposition of children's spirituality as a human phenomenon, anxieties concerning its inclusion in educational rhetoric might be somewhat dispelled, and that whilst it must be acknowledged that spirituality is part of religious expression, the two are not necessarily inextricably linked. As such, spiritual awareness, which I suggest is already evident through children's individual and collective experiences, might be recognised as an aspect of learning that is important to children, for their own well-being and their further engagement with the world.

My recommendation for policy makers then is that young children's spirituality is not evaded going forward but embraced as a significant aspect of Early Childhood Education. In consideration of the value placed on both nature and spirituality by many of the pioneers of education and care for young children, it is possible to suggest that the foundation for the inclusion of each in pedagogy is already laid, and as one reflects on the social situations within which the pioneers worked (McDowall Clark, 2020), even more than 100 years ago, it is not difficult to observe how similar situations, including poverty, ill-health, lack of opportunity or learning difficulties to name but a few, might be supported through a natural, spiritual pedagogy.

For teachers, I urge that when the hallmarks of spirituality as outlined in this book become manifest through children's play, responses, conversations or reflections, they are noticed. I also urge that they are then encouraged and identified in relation to what a child might be thinking, learning and acting on in that moment. Also, as Early Childhood pedagogy is still responsive to children's interests and ideas (albeit moving towards a more performative approach in many contexts), I suggest that teachers listen to how children are expressing themselves, especially in relation to their care for the world and others, to provide a framework within which they can express their feelings and put their thoughts into practice.

Research

Whilst the bank of literature relating to children's spirituality has grown over the past 30 years, with an increasing number of books and even doctoral theses addressing this subject, it is acknowledged by scholars and practitioners in the field (for example Adams et al., 2016; Mata-McMahon & Escarfuller, 2023), that more research is required in relation to the spirituality of young children, especially in non-religious environments. Equally, a range of texts are available to support practitioners in engaging children with nature (for example Waller et al., 2017; Walton, 2022); however, these texts, whilst significant, do not have both 'young children's spirituality and nature' as a focus. Rather, details are included that are relevant to (for example) Education for Sustainability within Early Childhood, or agency and voice; spirituality is included, but for a wider age group. Therefore, little is available with a focus on both.

There is also a lack of literature with philosophical depth and, whilst more recent texts (for example, Rouse, Hyde and Eaude, forthcoming) focus on the 'being' of children rather than their 'becoming,' in providing a rationale for the inclusion of spirituality within Early Childhood rhetoric and pedagogy, I would argue that this concerns spirituality 'in-itself' rather than the forward movement of spiritual awareness to action. Therefore, my recommendation to researchers would be to explore the relationship between spirituality and outdoor learning from an empirical perspective in order to gain data that might support the inclusion of both spirituality and nature within Early Childhood Education for the future. I also recommend that researchers draw on the work of Early Childhood pioneers and both recent and established theorists, but in so doing, as well as considering their pedagogical or practical outworking, also explore their philosophical perspectives so that the publications concerning both Early Childhood Education and Children's Spirituality are taken seriously within academia, and that empirical data gained from research has a robust underpinning.

Concluding comments

This publication concerns the inter-relationship between Early Childhood Education, spirituality and nature. It offers a reflection on how children's innate spirituality makes them prone to stand in awe in the outdoor environment while sustaining their sense of identity, connectedness and meaning-making. It also provides illustrations of how the environment has been seen to nurture and enhance young children's spirituality. Concerning the ontological and epistemological issues that are at the basis of Early Childhood pedagogy, the text is philosophical but practical, and where required, critical. By emphasising the importance of nature within pedagogy, it is hoped that this book has the potential to rekindle the conversation around the holistic development of children, and it is proposed that in relation to their experience of nature, young children's innate spirituality might indeed promote enhanced well-being and a sense of social responsibility.

References

Adams, K., Bull, L. & Maynes, M.L. (2016). Towards an understanding of the distinctive features of young children's spirituality. *European Early Childhood Education Research Journal*, 24(5), 760–774. https://doi.org/10.1080/1350293X.2014.996425

Eaude, T. (2020). *Identity, culture and belonging: Educating young children for a changing world*. London: Bloomsbury Academic.

Gandini, L. (1993). Connecting through caring and learning spaces. In C. Edwards, L. Gandini & G. Forman (Eds.), *The hundred languages of children: The Reggio Emilia approach to early childhood* (pp. 317). Norwood, NJ: Ablex Publishing Corporation.

Goodliff, G. (2016). Spirituality in early childhood education and care. In M. de Souza, J. Bone & J. Watson (Eds.), *Spirituality across disciplines: Research and practice* (pp. 67–80). Netherlands: Springer. https://doi.org/10.1007/978-3-319-31380-1

Heidegger, M. (1962). *Being and time*. Oxford: Blackwell Publishers.

Mata-McMahon, J. & Escarfuller, P. (2023). *Children's spirituality in early childhood education*. New York: Routledge. https://doi.org/10.4324/9781003081463

McDowall Clark, R. (2020). *Childhood in society for the early years*. 4th ed. London: Sage.

Robinson, C. (2019). Young children's spirituality: A focus on engaging with nature. *Australasian Journal of Early Childhood*, 44(4), 339–350. https://doi.org/10.1177/1836939119870907

Rouse, E., Hyde, B. & Eaude, T. (Eds.). (2024). *Nurturing young children as spiritual beings in a globalized world*. London: Bloomsbury Academic.

Tubbs, N. (2005). *The philosophy of the teacher*. Oxford: Blackwell Publishing.

Waller, T., Ärlemalm-Hagsér, E., Sandseter, E.B.H., Lee-Hammond, L., Lekies, K. & Wyver, S. (Eds.). (2017). *The Sage handbook of outdoor play and learning*. London: SAGE Publications.

Walton, C. (2022). *Childhood awaits every person*. London: Austin McCauley Publishers.

Index

Adams, K. 11, 16, 32
affordance 29
affordance theory (Gibson) 29, 60
Art as Experience (Dewey) 72
awareness 6, 27–28

Being 26–29, 86; *see also* potentiality-for-Being
Best, R. 45
bildung: creativity 79; dialectical approach 78; empower 80; ethical dilemma 78; interplay 79–80; learners 79; ontological foundation 78–79; pedagogical perspective 77; personal development 78–79; policy 78
Bilton, H. 42
biophilia 12, 33, 42
Birth to 5 Matters (2021) 49
Bleeksma, E. 63
Bone, Jane 18, 32, 50
Boumann, A. 63
Brie, J. 11
Bull, L. 11
Burnard, P. 37

Campbell-Barr, V. 44, 47
care 5, 16, 31–32, 42
Carroll-Meehan, C.J. 11
Cedillo, S. 64
Champagne, Elaine 28
Chancellor, B. 60
Chen, A. 43
Chen, Heqin 14
Chhetri, R. 42
child-centred pedagogy 83–84

children in nature 29, 84
children's spirituality literature: affordance 29–30; awareness 27–28; expressions 28; holistic development 29; learning 26–27; philosophical perspective 26; reflection and critical thinking 28; relational consciousness 26; state of being 26; universal 25; view of ontology 27–28
children's spirituality, outdoor space: awareness 6; care 5; corporeal experience 4–5; creativity 3; fascination 3; imagination 2, 5–6; individuality and connectedness 4; literature 5; overview 1–2; presence 2–3; synopsis 6–7
Cincera, J. 62
Coles, Robert 25, 26
concerning children's spirituality 85
corporeal experience 4–5
cosmo-centric spiritual sensitivity 33
Craft, A. 37
creativity 3, 36–37, 79
Cremin, T. 37
critical pedagogy approach 7; consciousness 76–77; dialectical approach 76–77; learning 74–76; ontological possibility 75; personal freedom 74
criticality: cultural and social inclusion 62–66; models fixed entities 66–67
Csikszentmihalyi, M. 35
Cullen, J. 32

cultural and social inclusion: constructing local epistemologies 64; decolonisation 64–65; ethnographic research 63–64; inclusion and decolonisation practice 64–66; language of inclusion 64; ontological connectedness 65; self-critical 62–63; socio-cultural pillar 63; Western individualisation 63

Da Silva, J.P. 15
Dasein 26–27, 70–71
decolonisation 64–65
Democracy and Education (Dewey) 72
Dewey, John 71–72, 74, 76, 79
Downes, G. 58
Dunne, L. 64

Early Childhood Education 6, 9, 11; *see also individual entries*
Early Childhood foundations: early childhood practice 48–49; nature in the work of early childhood pioneers 44–48; overview 41; pedagogical principles for nature and spirituality 49–51; synopsis 51; value of nature for young children 41–43
Early Childhood policy: overview 9; and practice 83–85; spiritual deficit in policy, United Kingdom 9–13; spiritual deficit in policy, USA, China, Hong Kong and wider 13–15; spiritually inclusive policy, Australia and New Zealand 15–20; synopsis 20–21
Early Childhood practice: criticality, cultural and social inclusion 62–66; criticality, models fixed entities 66–67; Eco-Schools 60–62; Education for Sustainable Development (ESD) 54–58; Forest School 58–60; overview 54; synopsis 67
Early Learning Curriculum Framework (New Zealand) 74

Early Years Foundation Stage Statutory Framework (2023) 10–12, 36
Eaude, T. 36–37, 84
eco-centric spiritual sensitivity 32–33
Eco-Schools 60–61; environmental issues 61–62; ESD 61; example of 61; food waste 62; Green Flag accreditation 61; recycling scheme 62
education 84; *see also individual entries*
Education Act (1988) 24
Education for Sustainable Development (ESD) 17, 34; 17 Sustainable Development Goals 55; being 56–57; capability-centred approach 56; children's rights 55; child's maturity 57; nature and social responsibility 54; sustainability 55–56
Education Reform Act 9
educational rhetoric 9, 11, 85
Elliott, S. 60
Else, P. 56
England 24
Erricker, C. 66
Erricker, J. 66
Escarfuller, P. 13, 26, 29, 32, 50

Farrugia, K. 30, 34
fascination 3
Featherbe, A. 56
Fisher, J. W. 14
flow 35
Forest School: Denmark 58; engage in risk-taking activities 59; environmentally responsible views 59; example of 60; illustration 60; mental health and well-being 58–59; pedagogical principles 59
frameworks of understanding: children's spirituality literature 25–30; the impact of spiritual experience 34–37; overview 24–25; spiritual identities 30–34; synopsis 37

Fraser, D. 18
Freire, P. 74, 75, 77, 79
Froebel, Friedrich 44

Garden, A. 58, 59
Gegeo, D. 64
Gellel, A.M. 30
Gelven, M. 27
Gergen, K. 32
Gifford, R. 43
Gillan, K. 63
Goodliff, G. 10–11, 36, 84
Grajczonek, J. 17
Greenfield, C.F. 18
Greenman, J. 41
Grenier, J. 49
guinea pig 5, 31

Hardy, Alister 25
Harris, Kathleen 36, 51
Hart, T. 27, 29
Hay, David 5, 26, 28, 35, 46
Hegel, G. W. F. 6, 66, 76–79
Heidegger, M. 26–28, 57, 70, 74–76, 79, 85
Helenius, A. 44
Hyde, B. 29, 32

imagination 2, 5–6, 35–36
impact of spiritual experience 34–35; creativity 36–37; imagination 35–36; presence 35
individuality and connectedness 4
'in-itself' 6, 66, 76, 78–79, 86
Isaacs, Susan 44, 47, 48

Keltner, D. 28
Kemp, N. 55, 56
Kerr, L. 11
kindergarten 44–45, 60–61
Kirmani, M.H. 30–33, 79
Kirmani, S. 30–33, 79
Knight, S. 59
Korkmaz, A. 61
Kroufek, R. 62

lack of literature 86
Last Child in the Woods (Louv) 43

Lau, G. 14
Lau, N.-S. 35
Lavin-Miles, Z. 54
The Lodge 1, 4–5, 73, 75
Louv, R. 43
Loveridge, J. 32
Luff, P. 54

magic moment 50
magic spots 50–51
Malaguzzi, Loris 30, 34, 48, 73, 84
Mata-McMahon, J. 13, 26, 29, 32, 50
Maynes, M. L. 11
McCreery, Elaine 28
McDowall Clark, R. 48
McMillan, Margaret 44, 47, 48
McMillan, Rachel 47
Mellor, S. 63
Miller, L. 31
Mirkovic, D. 20
Mitton, M. 36
models fixed entities 66–67
Montessori, Maria 44, 46, 71
Moss, S.M. 41

National Curriculum in England (2014) 9–10
nature in the work of early childhood pioneers: child-centred principles 44; connectedness 45; Isaac's pedagogy 48; kindergarten 44–45; Montessori's pedagogy 46–47; play 44–45; three forms of learning 44–45
nature, spirituality, and early childhood education *see individual entries*
New Zealand 74
Ng, D.T.K. 14, 15
Nikiforidou, Z. 54, 56, 58
Nordenbo, S.E. 78
Nugent-Jones, M. 11
Nxumalo, F. 64, 65
Nye, Rebecca 5, 26, 28, 35, 46

ontology 27, 70
Otto, Rudolph 28

pedagogical principles for nature and spirituality 49–51
pedagogy 11, 14, 46–48; being and potentiality-for-being 70–74; bildung 77–80; critical pedagogy 74–77; overview 70; synopsis 80–81
Pedagogy of the Oppressed (Freire) 74
Phenomenology of Spirit (Hegel) 66
Pokhrel, S. 42
Polemikou, A. 15
policy makers 15, 83–84; learning outdoors, full-time provision 84; meta-spaces of spirituality 84–85; physical and conceptual classroom 84; recommendation 84–85; spirituality in curriculum 85
potentiality-for-Being 57; affordance 73; *Dasein* 70–71; democracy 73; Dewey's philosophy 71–72; identity and encourages positive relationships 74; pedagogy 71; philosophy 71; potentiality 72; pre-ontology 70
Pramling Samuelsson, I. 34, 55, 57
presence 2–3, 35
publication concerns 86
Pytka, B. 20

Radesky, J. 43
recommendations for: overview 83; policy and practice 83–85; research 85–86; synopsis 86
Reggio, Emilia 30, 48
Reggio Emilia approach 30, 34, 48, 73
research 85–86
Robinson, C. 16, 17, 29, 30, 32
Rogoff, Barbara 63, 64
Rose, G. 77

Sachdev, G. 17
Schein, Deborah 28, 30, 32, 42, 49–50

School Inspection Handbook (Ofsted) 10
Schumacher, J. 43
Scott, D. 28, 35
self-critical 62–63
Sen, Amartya (1996) 56
senso-centric spiritual sensitivity 30–31
socio-centric spiritual sensitivity 31–32
The Spirit of the Child (Hay and Nye) 26
spiritual deficit in policy: United Kingdom 9–13; USA, China, Hong Kong and wider 13–15
Spiritual Development category 10
spiritual identities: cosmo-centric spiritual sensitivity 33; eco-centric spiritual sensitivity 32–33; ethical behaviour 34; framework 30; reflexivity and agency 34; senso-centric spiritual sensitivity 30–31; socio-centric spiritual sensitivity 31–32
The Spiritual Life of Children (Coles) 25
Spiritual, Moral, Social, and Cultural(SMSC) development 9–10
The Spiritual Nature of Man (Coles) 25
spiritually inclusive policy, Australia and New Zealand 15–20
Spontaneous Activity in Education (Montessori) 46–47
sustainability 55–56

Tang, F. 12–14
Tesar, M. 20
three meta-environments 35–36
Tiplady and Menter (2020) 59
Tregenza-May, S. 44
Tubbs, N. 71
Tyrell, N. 55

value of nature for young children:
  Being-in-the-world 42; benefits
  42; Covid-19 pandemic 42–43;
  interconnected 42; nature-deficit
  disorder 43; online resources 43;
  social and economic disparities
  41–42; universal and timeless 41
Vollans, C. 49
von Humboldt, Wilhelm 78

Wallbridge, Ruth 57
Walton, Christopher 50
Watson-Gegeo, Karen Ann 63

Webster, R. S. 71, 72
Wills, R. 11
Wilson, E. O. 29, 42, 50
Wolniakowska-Majewska, Z. 11
Woolley, R. 32

Yarwood, R. 55
Yildiz, T.G. 61
young children's learning 84

Zhang, K. 13
Zhao, J. 12–14
Zuckermann, B. 43

For Product Safety Concerns and Information please contact our EU
representative GPSR@taylorandfrancis.com
Taylor & Francis Verlag GmbH, Kaufingerstraße 24, 80331 München, Germany

www.ingramcontent.com/pod-product-compliance
Lightning Source LLC
Chambersburg PA
CBHW071513150426
43191CB00009B/1516